TRAILBLAZERS

TYNDALE
MOMENTUM®

A Tyndale nonfiction imprint

TRAILBLAZERS

MICAH E. DAVIS

A journey

to discover

God's purpose

for your life

Visit Tyndale online at tyndale.com.

Visit Tyndale Momentum online at tyndalemomentum.com.

Visit the author online at micahedavis.com.

Tyndale, Tyndale's quill logo, *Tyndale Momentum*, and the Tyndale Momentum logo are registered trademarks of Tyndale House Ministries. Tyndale Momentum is a nonfiction imprint of Tyndale House Publishers, Carol Stream, Illinois.

Trailblazers: A Journey to Discover God's Purpose for Your Life

Designed by Julie Chen

Published in association with the literary agency of The Steve Laube Agency.

For information about special discounts for bulk purchases, please contact Tyndale House Publishers at csresponse@tyndale.com, or call 1-855-277-9400.

Library of Congress Cataloging-in-Publication Data

A catalog record for this book is available from the Library of Congress.

ISBN 978-1-4964-7572-5

Printed in the United States of America

29	28	27	26	25	24	23
7	6	5	4	3	2	1

To Rylei.

May we forever blaze trails together
this side of heaven.

Contents

WHAT IS A TRAILBLAZER?

LIMINAL SPACE.

The space in-between.

At least, that's what I was told liminal space is.[1] Theodora Blanchfield defined liminal space as, "Be[ing] on the precipice of something new but not quite there yet."[2]

Brilliant.

My mentor used the imagery of an acrobat jumping from one bar to another: "The point between the release of one bar and the grasping of the next bar? That's liminal space."

The book you're about to read is a guide for living a life like no one else. In a cultural moment where we're "languishing"[3] (as *New York Times* writer Adam Grant put it), we must ask ourselves if we're doing what God requires of us to truly discover our God-given purpose.

Because *you* have a purpose.

God has uniquely equipped you, the one-of-a-kind you, to blaze a trail, to live a life that exemplifies Jesus, the ultimate Trailblazer, who himself is one of a kind.

But here's the question: Are you willing to persevere through the journey it takes to get there?

The character trek about to unfold typically progresses in liminal space. We see that thread all throughout Scripture, from Moses, to Rahab, and even to Jesus. We often remember the moment they embraced their identity as the Trailblazers God had called them to be, even as we tend to forget the many dark nights, lonely times, and seasons of desert obscurity they endured to get to that point. In fact, the journey of liminal space usually plays out in a cycle.

The Five Phases of Liminal Space

Liminal space often plays out in five key phases.

Phase 1: Obscurity

The Israelites spent *forty years* in the desert before inheriting the Promised Land.

Jesus spent *forty days* in the wilderness before stepping into the spotlight of public ministry.

After reading this, you might feel tempted to grasp immediately for your God-given dream. My advice?

Take a breath.

Know that God calls you to a "long obedience in the same direction,"[4] not a cheap climb to celebrity.

YouTube has numerous examples[5] of ordinary people who pretend to be war heroes to attain the acclaim, respect, and praise actual defenders of our country deserve. We call this "stolen valor."

Those of us who attempt to blaze trails of significance without doing real, significant work in the shadows risk falling into that trap.

Embrace obscurity.

Phase 2: Wrestling

Real wrestling with Jesus takes place in the desert or wilderness, where the existential questions of liminal space arise:

Who am I?

Why am I here?

What is my purpose?

When will I know?

How will I get there?

I wish I could offer you potent wisdom for answering those questions (perhaps another book for another day), but for right now, know that wrestling is a *good* thing. In the wrestling we gain a clear purpose from God.

Phase 3: Clarity

As we wrestle with God, we gain clarity. When we dig deep to the roots of difficult questions, God often meets us in our curiosity.

In the desert God told Moses to lead an exodus.

In the desert Jesus received vocational clarity on who he was and who he was *not*.

In the desert God shaped and formed Paul for his ministry.

Phase 4: Consecration

As we clarify our calling, consecration often becomes the next phase.

How do we set ourselves apart? How do we cleanse and purify our hearts and souls so that we may become all of whoever God has called us to be?

We meet our pursuer, Jesus, more quickly when we pursue him instead of being content only to have him chase after us.

Phase 5: Breakthrough

After consecrating ourselves, we position ourselves to see breakthrough.

On holy ground Moses received an invitation to lead people from slavery to freedom.

Out of holy water Jesus received confirmation of his God-given identity.

Holy hands touched Saul's face and healed his blindness.

In the holy spaces of life, where cleansing occurs, we often get clearance to blaze the trail.

Becoming a True Trailblazer

Do you want your life to mean something? Do you long for a life of substance, impact, and transformation? Do you desire to make a difference—with everything in you—to have an impact, to blaze a trail?

Me, too.

But that means embracing the cycle of liminal space. Ordinary people become true Trailblazers in the very ordinary, mundane, day-to-day moments.

Before you can blaze the trail, understand that you must form and develop the traits we're going to unpack in this book. When you step fully into your calling and find yourself trailblazing for Jesus, you will need to lean on these foundational qualities as pillars for your journey. Don't try to learn character on the fly!

If you already hold a position of influence, I hope and pray that this work enhances the already strong character you possess. Influence without character is a dangerous game.

I suspect, however, that you, like me, find yourself in a place of obscurity. If so, this journey has the potential to change your life. Why?

Because a Trailblazer gets formed and shaped *in the field*. Even there, you must willingly put in the required work. Then, when the time comes to step into your God-given dream, you'll be ready.

The obstacles you face today may only hint at what's to come. If you can't defeat and overcome those obstacles now, then you won't stand a chance when the lights turn bright and your platform rises. An elevated position of influence requires an elevated level of integrity.

I believe God has called you to great things. He may already have put a specific dream on your heart. If so, seize it! Embrace it! But recognize that if you lack the necessary character qualities, you'll find yourself fighting fire with gasoline. You will feel an overpowering temptation to stroke your ego, raise your status, and magnify your importance.

How much better to endure the slow, steady path of growth—to receive God's invitation to truly live—than to try to cheat your way to the top and end up cut down and tossed into the fire.[6] We build the path to significance through many steps of small obedience.

Walking Out the Five Phases

God calls *every* Trailblazer to a lifetime of service, to holiness, and to submission. And I do mean "every."

Would it surprise you to hear that the Lord has asked me (although "asked" may be too soft a word) to walk out these five phases of liminal space in real time through the process of writing this book?

I originally thought the pages ahead would have a reflective focus. But over the past many months, God has deepened and sharpened each of the character attributes that I intended to highlight. And I discovered that some of these character attributes are mere inches deep in my own heart and soul. You will quickly see that I do not have it all together or have everything figured out!

But God, in his kindness, has decided to take me on a journey that has forced me to lean on these very words I'm going to offer. I've learned that it's a lot easier to cheer others on in the journey toward trailblazing than to walk it out myself.

Now, this shouldn't have surprised me. Why *wouldn't* the Lord ask me to go first before writing a book about my conviction that Trailblazers are people who go first?

Over the course of the last year, the Lord has made it clear that he's calling my wife, Rylei, and me into the unknown. And so, together, we are stepping out. As I write these words, I still don't know the full story or see the whole picture regarding the trail he's asked us to blaze. But here's what I do know:

God calls us to faithfulness.

God calls us to obedience.

God calls us to trust him.

God asks for our primary allegiance.

And so, Rylei and I are blazing a trail right alongside you.

Do you long to accept such a divine call, tailored by God to fit your own makeup, interests, and context? Do you want to be a Trailblazer? If so, know that it will set you apart—but not for *your* glory. Only Christ gets the credit in this lifestyle!

And the best part?

That's exactly how it's supposed to be.

I'll see you on the trail.

1

BUILD A FOUNDATION OF INTEGRITY

Character

I LIKE ORDER.

Whether that comes from my type A extremism or a compulsive necessity for organization, "order" keeps the world going 'round for me.

Everything on my desk—both in my study at the church and at home—has a place. I've color-coded the articles in my closet. My shoes sit in rows based on type. Even my junk drawer, the space where all random objects go to their unashamed grave, is, well . . . *ordered*.

So, imagine how hard I find it to begin a book *out* of order. While my story of discovering what it means to be a Trailblazer begins in Genesis, it doesn't start at the beginning.

Let me explain.

An Unexpected Key

Years ago, six months into my first full-time ministry stint, I found myself floundering. I had used up all the knowledge I had gained in Bible school, exhausted all the quick tips and techniques I had gathered from studying my parents (both pastors), and began running toward an uncomfortable reality:

I have no idea what I'm doing.

It haunted me. I didn't know what to do or where to go next. So, I sat down with my pastor to discuss options. He'd served in youth ministry for more than twenty years prior to his current role. Surely, he'd know what to do!

My mind grew excited at the prospect of our meeting. I started to imagine how great our time together would be. I began gathering materials for the greatest strategy meeting since Steve Jobs and Jony Ive conceived the iPhone.

I brought an outrageously expensive planner that could predict the next ten years of my life (not really, but it should have for the price); a massive, full-year wall calendar; six colored Expo markers (color-coding for the win); and my laptop—because, let's be honest, when all is said and done, it all goes in the iCal, anyway.

I sat down in his office, excited and anxious to get started. He would tell me *everything* I needed to do to shepherd our community well! And I felt ready to conceptualize it all, to the last detail, for the next calendar year.

Instead, he issued me a challenge that altered the course of my life.

"Micah, have you ever heard of a vision day?"

"Is that like, a staff retreat? The start of a capital campaign?"

"No, a vision day is a day to retreat and get alone with God and to ask him for fresh vision in your life and ministry. It's a day to be quiet and still. To spend unhurried time with him to allow him to infuse inspiration and innovation into your soul."

Huh?

I had never thought of that. I slowly began rolling up my massive Expo calendar. A day—alone—with God? Sounded wholly unnecessary and unproductive. But I was willing to give it a try.

So, on a random Friday in November, I cleared my schedule and reserved a room at an off-site business. I had nothing on the table but a journal, a Bible, and a pen. I prayed and asked God for fresh vision of the type of life he wanted me to live (and to call our community to live). I said amen and opened his Word and began reading. A few hours later, I came across Joseph's story and this verse in particular: "And now, do not be distressed and do not be angry with yourselves for selling me here, because it was to save lives that God sent me ahead of you."[1]

Something about this line stopped me in my tracks. In the quiet and in the stillness of that holy space, God impressed a word upon my heart which began a journey that brought us here:

Trailblazers.

That's who God is calling our community to be. That's who God is calling me to be. A Trailblazer.

But first, I needed to find out more about this Joseph guy. Why had God sent him ahead to blaze a trail and to save the lives of others?

A Story of Cycles

Joseph's story comes on the heels of three patriarchal biographies of Israel, God's chosen nation. Abraham, Isaac (Abraham's son), and Jacob (Isaac's son) became the forefathers of God's nation. With these three men and their families, God set in motion the redemptive story of his people.

Joseph was the second youngest of Jacob's twelve sons. And you think you have it rough in your family? Imagine having ten highly competitive older brothers!

Joseph was a miracle baby, of sorts. Dad had him long after he thought he'd finished having children. Also, Joseph was the son of Rachel, Jacob's favorite wife, who until that point could not have children. (Yes, Jacob had a favorite wife; reason #36 why having multiple wives is so wrong.)

The birth of Joseph elated Jacob. He transferred his favoritism of Rachel to their son, as the Bible explains: "Now [Jacob] loved Joseph more than any of his other sons, because he had been born to him in his old age; and he made an ornate robe for him."[2]

Jacob showered Joseph with favor, even giving his young son a swaggy[3] (Gen Z translation for "ornate," meaning elaborate or decorated)[4] robe to wear while taking care of Dad's sheep. As you might imagine, Joseph's brothers did not appreciate the swaggy gift.

Joseph didn't help his caucse when he followed up the robe ceremony by enthusiastically overdetailing two dreams he'd had,[5] which featured the sun, moon, and stars bowing down to him (as did some sheaves of grain, whatever those are).

Both dreams painted a picture of Joseph's family *bowing down* to him. Joseph's angry brothers did not receive his dreams any better than they did his coat. Between the robe and the dreams, Joseph's brothers' hatred toward him reached a boiling point. While in the field shepherding one day, Joseph's brothers devised a plan to kill Joseph.

(Again: You think you have it rough in your family?)

Thankfully, one brother spoke up and persuaded his siblings to reexamine their options.[6] They decided to throw Joseph into a dry well and leave him there for dead. Thank goodness! (My first run at sarcasm, okay?)

During a casual sit-down for lunch after abandoning their brother to die, they saw some merchants in the distance. And then another brother came up with a brilliant idea: "What will we gain if we kill our brother and cover up his blood? Come, let's sell him to the Ishmaelites and not lay our hands on him; after all, he is our brother, our own flesh and blood."[7]

All the brothers present agreed.

So. Much. Better (continuing the sarcasm trend).

They sold Joseph for pennies on the dollar and the slave traders whisked him away to Egypt, where he faced a myriad of bad circumstances, poor luck, and divine favor. The odd cycle continued in Joseph's life for almost ten years.

When a powerful Egyptian official named Potiphar bought Joseph, the young Hebrew slave found such favor with him that Potiphar eventually put Joseph in charge of his entire household. With Joseph at the helm, Potiphar's house flourished.

Then one day, Potiphar's wife made a sexual advance toward Joseph, which he quickly rejected. Humiliated, Potiphar's wife accused Joseph of attempted rape, which forced Potiphar to throw Joseph in prison.[8]

So ended *Cycle One*. Joseph had gone from beloved and favored slave to outcast and forgotten prisoner.

While in prison, Joseph befriended the king's ex-cupbearer and baker, who both had been thrown in prison for offending the king (called Pharaoh). Joseph saw their distress, asked them about it, and heard they'd both had strange, unsettling dreams the night before. He offered to interpret those dreams. He had good news for the cupbearer, not so much for the baker.[9]

Joseph, sensing his fortune turning, asked the cupbearer to remember him when he came before Pharaoh as a free man.

Joseph's interpretation of the dream came true, and the cupbearer appeared before Pharaoh. Only, the cupbearer forgot all about Joseph. And Joseph's unjustified stay in prison continued. *Cycle Two*.

Languishing in prison for roughly another two years, Joseph remained a man of integrity and eventually got promoted to overseeing all the prisoners. At that point, Pharaoh himself started having dreams. When searching for interpreters, Pharaoh jogged the memory of the cupbearer, who recommended Joseph as a possible seer. Pharaoh agreed.

And here the cycle broke down.

Joseph came before Pharaoh, interpreted his dreams, and devised a plan for how to take advantage of the mixed future he foresaw. Pharaoh loved it so much that he made Joseph second-in-command over the entire nation.[10]

That's what we call a comeback, folks.

Joseph quickly got Egypt rolling. For seven years, God blessed the nation, which Joseph took full advantage of by creating storehouses for the excess grain produced. Joseph knew that a seven-year famine was coming. When that famine eventually hit, surrounding nations began to starve—but not Egypt, because of Joseph's insight. Egypt kept rolling along and even had enough to aid the surrounding starving nations . . . including people from the land of Canaan (aka Joseph's family).

One day Joseph's brothers strolled into town, looking for food, and came face to face with Joseph. Joseph immediately clubbed one brother on the jaw and uppercut the youngest on the chin . . . Okay, maybe the story doesn't go exactly like that.

The brothers didn't recognize Joseph, due to his massive change in appearance (he looked like an Egyptian) and older age. It'd been more than twenty years, remember?

Through some playful deception and innocent payback, Joseph worked his brothers through an up-and-down emotional roller coaster, making them *really* work to receive their share of food. Consider it Joseph's way of processing his hurt and pain.

Eventually, Joseph came clean before his brothers, revealing that he was their long-forgotten brother. And then, the craziest thing happened . . .

Joseph's brothers *bowed down* to Joseph.[11]

Remember that long-ago dream that made Joseph's brothers angry enough to kill him, and then led them to sell him into slavery? Yeah, it comes true. So much for being cast away as "that dreamer." Joseph was a prophet.

The story ends with family reunions, happy tears, and a restored relationship between Joseph and his father, Jacob. All is well with the world, and Joseph perfectly sums up the journey in Genesis 45: "Do not be distressed and do not be angry with yourselves for selling me here, because it was to save lives that God sent me ahead of you."[12]

Joseph then reassures his brothers, "You intended to harm me, but God intended it for good to accomplish what is now being done, the saving of many lives."[13]

In this story we discover the true essence of a Trailblazer, as well as why our story must begin with Joseph. Throughout all of Joseph's life—amidst bad circumstances, in seasons of divine favor, and in instances of horrendous fortune—one thing remains steady and intact: his *character*.

The Core of a Trailblazer

Character lies at the very core of a Trailblazer.

Without character, all other commendable traits falter and wither. Character creates an environment ripe for God to work in us and through us.

From a young age, the idea of character has captivated me. Perhaps it has fascinated you too. Character is why we love going to the movies, reading books, or watching TV. The entertainment industry bases almost all its stories around heroes or heroines who find themselves: A) in difficult circumstances; B) facing adversity; or

C) on a mission to fulfill (something like Joseph). The *character* of these heroes and heroines determines whether they succeed.

Perhaps more than most, heroes riveted me. *I* wanted to be the hero.

At three years of age, I swung (jumped) from tree to tree (couch to chair) in my Fruit of the Loom underwear, roaring like an ape and doing my best impersonation of Tarzan.

At age eight, my brother Elijah and I got swept up in the craze of *Spy Kids* and dressed as agents for three straight trick or treat outings.

Even through high school and college, the allure and appeal of the Marvel Universe overwhelmed me as I saw *myself* in many of those heroes.

Why?

Character attracts us. Difficult circumstances either reveal the very best or expose the very worst of who we are. Character polarizes and captivates. *Merriam-Webster* defines character as "moral excellence and firmness."[14]

James Merritt, in his illuminating work on character, says it this way: "Character is the impression your life leaves on others."[15] Makes sense, doesn't it?

There's a reason I watch Captain America maintain his composure when chaos breaks out around him. I leave the theater wanting to become more composed.

It's why I read Joseph's story and want to be a man of integrity in the face of temptation.

It's why we all grow up with "heroes" or "role models" whom we strive to mirror in our words, actions, and habits.

Character is the core element in the life of a Trailblazer. It encompasses all the other wonderful traits we'll talk about. It breeds an essence or a disposition of quiet strength that attracts others and pulls them in.

While a life of character is worth building, however, few seem willing to blaze that path. The jungle of life can feel intense, scary, treacherous, and downright demoralizing. But a Trailblazer has such a solid character that the dangers of the jungle don't stand a chance. To blaze trails previously untraveled, one must possess a strength of character that will stand up to and overcome all the dangers of the wilderness.

Character provides the foundation of every Trailblazer.

Put to the Test

My own character got put to the test when I was eleven years old. A new movie titled *Benchwarmers* had just released on DVD, starring one of my favorite actors of all time: Jon Heder, more famously known as Napoleon Dynamite.

Earlier that year, as a new student from a different town, I had been chosen as student body president by my fifth-grade class, after attending school there for only three weeks. You might think, *Wow, you must've been an incredible kid of character whom your peers respected and looked up to!*

I wish I could nod my head, but in fact, I had won over (bribed) my classmates with an ingenious marketing campaign spearheaded by my ruthless campaign manager and primary investor (my dad) and inspired by the heroes of my life at the time: Napoleon and Pedro (Efren Ramirez). We called my campaign, "Vote for Micah."

I had shirts printed, buttons made, and I even gave my entire fifth-grade class free tater tots if they voted for me (no rules prohibited this, okay? Don't judge me). It worked and my love for Napoleon Dynamite became forever etched in my heart and soul.

But back to my character.

When *Benchwarmers* released, I knew that I *had* to see it.

"Dad," I said, "it has *Napoleon Dynamite* in it!"

I didn't know that *Benchwarmers* was no *Napoleon Dynamite*. My parents didn't see it as an appropriate movie for an eleven-year-old to watch.

I fumed and fussed for weeks. But then, it released on DVD. My friend, Dustin, aided by his hedonistic parents (I'm kidding!), obtained *Benchwarmers* . . . and it just so happened that I planned to attend a sleepover at Dustin's house that Friday night.

On the docket for the night? *Benchwarmers*.

I'll never forget how nervous I felt when they pressed play on the main menu. While the other boys in the room could hardly contain their excitement, I felt terrified. I wouldn't eat or drink anything. My mouth went dry. I kept looking over my shoulder, just waiting for the ghost of my parents to snatch my soul right out of my chair. I tried to laugh at the funny parts and sweat profusely during the inappropriate scenes. I had blatantly disobeyed my parents . . . and my guilt felt overpowering.

When I returned home the next day, I felt shell-shocked. I knew I needed to tell my dad, but I couldn't face him. So, I pretended like nothing bothered me. A few hours later, though, I'd had enough. I needed to confess.

I remember walking into my dad's bedroom as he watched TV and asking if I could talk to him. As soon as he turned off the set, my tears flooded. I confessed how I'd disobeyed his command to not watch that movie, how I'd lied about watching another movie, and how guilty I felt for exposing myself to something I never should have seen.

He responded with tenderness and warmth. Without anger, he said, "Don't you see now that we weren't saying you couldn't watch it because we're mean, but because we wanted to protect your eyes, ears, and heart from things that were inappropriate for your age?"

I told him I understood (but did NOT tell him how good a dad he was).

Why is character so important?

When we disregard or disobey the commandments of our heavenly Father, we hurt no one more than we hurt ourselves. The guilt and shame that pummels us can feel unbearable. The lies and insecurities that Satan can implant in our heads both stunts our growth and even prevents us from producing the character we need to step back safely into the wilderness of the world. Merritt puts it this way: "Low character comes at a high cost."[16]

So, while I really like order, I love character more. Which is why the life of a Trailblazer must begin with building a foundation of character—and that requires time, temperance, and commitment. We must willingly make the right decisions, do the right things, say the right words at the right times, and then *do that* over and over and over again. Building character isn't sexy or glamorous. But when character fails, spectacular collapses often follow. The world feasts on those downfalls, made even worse by all the glitz and glamor.

How does the quote go? "Trust is built in drops and lost in buckets." The same goes for character. We build it in drops and lose it in buckets.

Character matters.

As I forge ahead in life and ministry, I've begun to recognize the crucial place of character with respect to my specific vocation. I'm a pastor. I would hope (especially if you know me personally) that this might warm your heart. Maybe you've prayed over me, prayed with me, or received prayer from me. In a sense, our words over one another have helped to shape and form our character. What a gift to be invited into the most intimate spaces of people's lives!

But I also know that you might see that "pastor" line and cringe.

Oh, here we go. Another hotshot young preacher who thinks he's the stuff. Another guy with big names backing him and smooth words covering him. A charismatic communicator now writing books? Yeah, like we've never seen that before.

To you, I say: you're right. I totally get it. The role I've accepted doesn't have a great recent track record and the latest headlines only make it worse. My pastoral legacy as a tattooed, nose-pierced, young, relatively fit white guy conjures up images of scandal, coercion, and abuse.

Believe me, I'm aware of it.

I'm ashamed to say that some men after whom I modeled my ministry probably come to mind when you think of "wolves in sheep's clothing." But please hear me: that is *not* the trail I long to blaze. In fact, my ambition has shifted from becoming the hero to becoming the guide, the highest calling I can imagine for any pastor.

God never meant for his church to put pastors on a pedestal. Pastors don't need always to be front and center, and certainly we must not worship or idolize them. That you are reading this book is an honor and privilege I do not deserve. No one owes it to me as my "right."

Did you know that the word *pastor* doesn't even appear in the New Testament? The translators of the Geneva Bible back in 1560 (fifty-one years before the King James version appeared) had to translate the Greek word *poimenas* from Ephesians 4:11 into English, and they had two options: *pastor* (Latin) and *shepherd* (Middle English). They chose the Latin term and set a precedent that remains even today . . . but probably not without some cost. The word *shepherd* instead recalls Davidic language, don't you think?

God has called me to be in the field with you, to help you on the journey toward becoming the Trailblazer God has called you to be. That, in essence, is what I hope this book is: a tool from a guide who longs to see you flourish.

While this book highlights some things God has done in me, please know, it's not about me. Also, I need you to know that this work is not a pastime. These are not, "the things I've learned and am now ready to pass on to others." While God planted certain character attributes in me decades ago, all of them still are and always will be *in process* in my life.

Just as they will be in yours.

That is the life of apprenticeship to Jesus.

Does the Trail Beckon?

If you believe God has placed a calling on your life, or if you feel as though you're destined to change the world, or if you have a dream to impact society unlike anyone's dream before you, then please hear me: YOU CAN! I believe in you.

More importantly, so does God. Whatever he's called you to do, he will see you through.[17]

But while the journey toward reaching whatever goal, dream, or aspiration you have is simple—love God and others—it is *not* easy.

You will face trials and troubles, temptations of all kinds, unjust and unfair rulings, bad breaks, terrible luck, a bad draw, kicks to the face and side, stabs in the back. It all lies ahead. The wilderness is not for the faint of heart!

The wilderness is calling, however, even beckoning to those with a trail to blaze. And with God, that trail is worth blazing. On the other side of your fear, you'll find your future. On the other side of your pain, you'll discover the promise that God has etched onto your heart.

Thank goodness that we have a Shepherd who epitomized what real character looks like!

Now, with a foundation of character established, we have what it takes to enter the wild life of a Trailblazer.

2

TAKE THE FIRST STEP
Initiative

I'LL NEVER FORGET the moment I stepped off that 100-foot-tall platform.

My heart stopped. Everything around me seemed to stand still. I felt trapped in a moment of terror unlike anything I'd ever experienced.

And why was I about to step off a 100-foot-tall platform into an abyss in the first place? Let's rewind and set the scene.

I'm twelve years old and petrified of heights. My dad thinks it's a good idea to attend a father-son camp with me and my two younger brothers, featuring a weekend of eating meat, playing basketball, throwing axes, shooting paintball, and engaging in a battle called "crud wars."

You know . . . "dude" stuff.

Here's the thing. My brothers and I take after my dad in the sense that none of us are a "man's man." I can count on one hand the number of times we've shot a gun or gone to the bar for a drink.

The only sort of hunting we've done has been for deals at the mall. Oh, and I never want to relive the *one* time we tried camping the *right* way.

Understand that we are *not* outdoorsy adrenaline junkies; nor are we the adventurous type. While this fact made our macho-man's weekend rather uncomfortable, it accentuated a deep-seated fear churning in the depths of my heart.

The unknown.

It began as a simple jab from one of my brothers: "I bet you won't do the zip line."

"I bet you I will!"

I had other, braver men to impress.

And yet, that entire journey to the top of the platform turned into a constant thought stream of doubt.

You don't have what it takes.

This is unsafe.

You're going to die.

I know, I know, it's just a zip line; but my fear of heights poured gas on the very real insecurities of my soul.

What if you're not enough?

What if you get out of control?

What if you fail?

The moment I stepped off that platform into the void became a picture of many-to-come crossroad moments in my life.

Every great feat that anyone has accomplished began with a choice. A choice to start the first experiment, run the first lap, ask the first question, provide the first answer. A choice to take the first step.

Once a Trailblazer establishes a foundation of character in his or her life, that individual must decide what this life will amount to. During the formative moments of life, questions arise:

Do I matter?

What's my purpose?

Will I be remembered?

We *long* to matter. We long for *meaning*. But how do we matter or find that meaning? As the adage goes, "You'll never know unless you try."

On the other side of a Trailblazer's initiative lies a life of meaning, purpose, and legacy. An adventure of a lifetime! We have many examples in Scripture of individuals who could testify to this.

But *we* still have to jump. *We* still have to take the first step . . . which brings me to our first character attribute: *initiative*.

I'd like to introduce you to Abram.

From Unfaith to Faith

Abram's trailblazing journey begins in Genesis 12.[1]

I'm fascinated by the interaction described there. Out of nowhere, "The Lord" appears to Abram. Why did I put, "The Lord" in quotation marks? We'll come back to that.

The Lord gives Abram a command to blaze a trail: "Go from your country . . . to the land I will show you."[2]

Blaze the trail, Abram!

God then follows up his command with a promise: Blaze the trail and I will bless you. I'll make you into a great nation. I'll bless those who bless you and curse those who curse you. All people on earth will be blessed through you.[3]

A pretty sweet deal, no?

Then, the real crazy starts. Abram obeys: "So Abram went, as the LORD had told him . . ."[4]

If you've read the Bible for any length of time, this may feel like a typical interaction between God and one of his Trailblazers. But we need to put this interaction into context to fully understand and appreciate it.

Throughout our time on earth, we face what I'll call "fork-in-the-road" decisions. Many of these are societally accepted and normal: Which college will I attend? Which person will I marry? What career will I pursue?

Others are more unexpected: Will I live with Mom or Dad after the bottom falls out? Do I tell the police what happened or stay silent? How will I make that difficult relationship decision?

At this point, certain unhealthy motivations pop up. You'll see them appear time and again throughout our time together. These unhealthy motivations drive us to make poor, ungodly, and often disastrous decisions.

I see two types of such motivators: heavenly ones and worldly ones. Heavenly motivators push us toward becoming more whole, while worldly motivators seek to rip apart our souls.

Our motivators determine our fork-in-the-road moments in life. How do we discover a life of purpose? A life that matters? A life that others remember? Will such a life be driven by selfish ambition and greed, or will we develop a life of substance based on obedience, submission, and faith?

Life is a series of decisions, both planned and unexpected, hopeful and heart-wrenching, joyous and maddening. How do we choose which direction to go?

We find Abram right here . . . only he's already lived his life.

Did I forget to mention that Abram is already seventy-five years old when this conversation takes place?[5] Today, we think that someone at that age deserves to be sipping mai tais poolside somewhere warm and south.[6]

But God is just getting started with Abram.

He tells Grandpa Abram that, should he begin blazing this trail, he'll serve as the starting point for God's chosen people and nation, Israel.

Just one more issue: Grandpa Abe has no kids.

No kids = no descendants = no nation = *big* problem.

And yet, God tells this elderly man that he'll be the "Father of many nations."[7]

Abram? The seventy-five-year-old with no kids? The father of many nations? Is that not outrageous to you? It certainly is to me. And it was to Abram and his wife too.

Twenty-five years pass after this conversation and still, no traditional heir.[8] At this point, the divine promise of becoming a "father of many nations" feels like a pipe dream. It feels like one of those moments where one laughs so as not to cry. Oh, wait—that's actually what happens: "Abraham fell facedown; he laughed and said to himself, 'Will a son be born to a man a hundred years old? Will Sarah bear a child at the age of ninety?'"[9]

Sarah later apparently took a cue from her husband and said, "God has brought me laughter, and everyone who hears about this will laugh with me."[10]

Have you ever found yourself with what feels like a God-given dream? Have you been in a season where it feels as though God has promised something to you: A ring? A baby? A promotion? An achievement?

But it hasn't come.

I have.

As I've reflected on those moments throughout my life, however, I've realized that many times God has not denied the fruition of some dream; my own agency has done that. Agency is simply God's gift to us to be able to *choose*.

Can you say the same thing?

"I feel like God's given me a dream to get married." And yet, you've never worked up the courage to ask her out.

"I feel like God's called me to be a CEO of a Fortune 500 company." And yet, you've never shown up to work early a day in your life.

"I feel like God's calling me to be a doctor or dentist." And yet, you haven't even submitted applications for your undergraduate studies.

We need to realize that God *always* upholds his end of a promise. We see this throughout Scripture. His ultimate promise, the redemption of humanity, was made possible by the arrival of Jesus Christ. And hundreds of promises leading up to the Savior's birth happened too.[11]

A Trailblazer refuses to live in regret, but instead says "yes," takes initiative, and in humility, moves toward whatever dream God has set forth. At the inner core of a Trailblazer lies a supernatural courage, strength, and faith to go *first*. To take the first step in the direction of the trail to be blazed.

Abram followed this pattern. He literally went first, with no precedent to rely on. He couldn't open the Bible and read about individuals like himself because neither the Bible nor these individuals had yet come into existence.

I can hear someone saying, "Yeah, okay, Micah. Easy for you to say. Abram may not have had a Bible, but God spoke audibly (we presume) to him. How's that fair?"

If Abram had a clue as to who God was, maybe I'd give that to you. But here's the thing: Abram had *no idea* who God was. Check out these words from Joshua: "Thus says the LORD, the God of Israel, 'Long ago, your fathers lived beyond the Euphrates, Terah, the father of Abraham and of Nahor; and they served other gods.'"[12]

Did you catch that? They served *other* gods.

Remember earlier when I put "The LORD" in quotations? That's probably how Abram encountered God in the first place. I imagine he felt a little bit of skepticism when "The LORD" first spoke to him. Why wouldn't he? He served other gods at that point in his life. What would make this god any different?

This God was different because this God made a promise, in fact, a covenant. In Hebrew, the word we translate as "covenant" is *berit,* which means, "a contract."[13] God made three of them with Abram:

1. God will make Abram into a great nation.[14]

2. God will give Abram's descendants all the land from the Nile River to the Euphrates River (otherwise known as the Promised Land).[15]

3. God will make Abram the "father of many nations" and will give "the whole land of Canaan" (Promised Land) to his descendants.[16]

And guess what? God comes through on

Every.

Single.

One.[17]

This should come as no surprise, for this God prides himself on his faithfulness. Five times in Genesis 12:1-3, God says, "I will."

I will show you.

I will make you into a great nation.

I will make your name great.

I will bless.

I will curse.

The question then becomes, "Will you, Abram, trust and obey me? Will you jump? Will you take the first step?"

Not a Smooth Journey

Abram jumps, but he doesn't have the smoothest journey.

In fact, he suffers a lot of bumps along the way. Some things remain outside of his control (as in a quarter century of waiting), but most are in his control.

Take, for instance, the deception he engineered regarding his wife, Sarai—not once, but twice.[18] Then, there's the inclusion of a particular individual on the journey. Remember Genesis 12:1? "Go from your country, your people and your father's household . . ."

This is God saying, "Go blaze the trail, Abram."

Abram obeys . . . but he does much of the beginning stages of the journey on his own terms.

Confused? Let me explain.

After God and Abram's chat, it says that "Abram went, as the LORD had told him; and Lot went with him."[19]

Ah, missed that the first time around, didn't you? Oftentimes, we gloss over these seemingly minute details in the text, but they matter. So, let's just acknowledge the elephant in the room . . . who's Lot?

Lot is Abram's nephew. And Lot becomes nothing but trouble and inconvenience in Abram's life. First, Abram must divide his estate and surrender land to Lot because their current living conditions can't sustain both families.[20] Then, after separating, Lot gets captured and Abram must go on an Ethan Hunt, *Mission Impossible*-style mission to rescue him[21] (at least, that's how I imagine it).

Then, in another action-packed rescue mission, Abram attempts to save the city of Sodom and Gomorrah—unsuccessfully—and Lot's wife dies in the process.[22] And finally, as if it can't get any worse, Lot's family line continues through incestuous relationships with his two daughters.[23]

So, who's Lot?

Well . . . let's just say his inclusion is a big part (and source) of pain, anguish, and sorrow of Abram's journey.

And then there's the saga of Ishmael and Hagar,[24] antiquity's version of *Jerry Springer*. Ishmael's birth caused huge amounts of dissension, bitterness, and anger between Hagar and Sarai that lasted for years to come.

Okay. . . deep breath.

The life of a Trailblazer begins with a foundation of character and the journey starts when you say *yes* to the invitation God extends to you. The journey begins when you take the initiative to join God in the story he wants to write in you and through you. In other words, *how* you obey matters.

Abram provides a prime example of this. In the last couple of pages, we've dissected how Abram:

A. Tried to lie his way into safety.

B. Miserably included his nephew in the journey to prosperity.

C. Stepped outside the bond of his marriage to try to expedite the succession process.

Do you see it? This is all about trying to maintain control.

Where do you find yourself in your own trailblazing journey with God? Perhaps God has put a dream on your heart, and you've said yes! You're willing to go first, to blaze the trail, to step off the ledge and into the abyss of the unknown. Yet, you're doing so while clinging to the control panels of your life, hoping that you can manipulate your way into the life you dream about having.

You're doing so while clinging to that unhealthy person whom you feel provides security.

You're doing so while holding onto that destructive addiction that you feel provides comfort.

You're blazing a trail, just one moving in the opposite direction of the way God instructed you to go—all encumbered by the desire for control. And in the process, you're missing out on experiencing the fullness and richness of God's mercy, grace, and undeserved blessing.

Or maybe you're trying to beat the system in hopes that you can spin a fleeting flash of fame on TikTok or Twitter into the influence you need to bring people to Jesus.

Don't act like you haven't prayed about it!

As my mentor often asks, "What's the thing beneath the thing?"[25] What's driving you to blaze the trail? Is it to get famous? To have someone beautiful on your hip? To finally show him you're worth it?

Whatever the case, here's the reality: your desire for control will inhibit your ability to receive the full blessing of God.

Think about it. Abram's lie helped him accrue a mountain of wealth. Abram's inclusion of Lot granted him some security and familiarity for his journey into the unknown. Abram's sexual escapade with a female slave gave him the son he'd always wanted.

But it wasn't enough.

It'll *never* be enough. Why not? Because it wasn't done God's way.

In his kindness and mercy, God allows Abram, despite his lust for control, to experience wealth, security, pleasure, and fulfillment. But Abram misses out on *so* much more.[26]

Maybe you've accrued your followers, hooked up with that guy, aced that exam, or made your first million. Yet, you're still asking, "Is this all there is?"

Perhaps the most beautiful trait of God is his relentless pursuit and love of us. Despite Abram's mistakes, despite his recklessness, despite his pride, God continued to show up and give him further chances.

Genesis 17 is the perfect case study for this. At the ripe age of ninety-nine, Abram faces another fork in the road. Twenty-four years after the initial blessing and covenant, Abram returns to God broken, bruised, and battered from trying to live life his own way. Yet, God's affirming tone immediately makes itself evident: "Walk before me faithfully and be blameless. Then I will make my covenant between me and you and will greatly increase your numbers."[27]

In other words, he's saying, "It's a new day, Abram. I'm about to take the initiative for you. At one hundred years old, with your body, 'as good as dead,'[28] I will fulfill the promise through you. In fact, this is a new beginning for you. I'm changing your name! You'll now be called Abraham, which means, 'father of many nations.'" And then, God, with a strike of déjà vu, repeats the blessing from Genesis 12 almost verbatim, but with a stronger emphasis on the influence Abraham will have ("kings will come from you").[29]

Are you stunned yet?

God then reaffirms this covenant with Abraham, only this time, he asks Abraham to put a little skin in the game (I'm sorry, I had to). He tells Abraham that the physical sign of this covenant will be the procedure of circumcision, to serve as a constant reminder of the promise they both were committed to keeping.[30]

It keeps getting better (and don't worry, the gross part is over).

Genesis 17:15-16 says, "God also said to Abraham, 'As for Sarai your wife, you are no longer to call her Sarai; her name will be Sarah. I will bless her and will surely give you a son by her. I will bless her so that she will be the mother of nations; kings of peoples will come from her.'"[31]

God redeems and renames Sarah, too, extending to her the same extralavish blessing (mother of nations, kings of peoples will come from her). And how did Abraham respond?

> Abraham fell facedown; he laughed and said to himself, "Will a son be born to a man a hundred years old? Will Sarah bear a child at the age of ninety?" And Abraham said to God, "If only Ishmael might live under your blessing!"[32]

Do you see Abraham *still* trying to control the narrative? "This is crazy, God! A son? I'm one hundred years old! I can't have a son with Sarah. Can't we just give the blessing to Ishmael?" But that's not the trail God had called Abraham to blaze. He tasked Abraham with becoming the father of God's chosen people, who could come only through him and Sarah.

Maybe you feel as though the dream God has placed on your heart is too crazy. Perhaps you've tried to bargain with God or simply make the dream come true by your own strength. Maybe you've even tried to enter into an exchange agreement: "I'll give you this, God, if you don't make me do this."

Whatever the case, what if God is gently asking you to stop and to fully surrender? To give up control? What if this is the moment when you decide you'll be all in on blazing the trail God's called you to?

You may think, *It's too late for me, Micah. I'm a lost cause. You don't know what I've done. You can't possibly understand my situation.*

Um, hello? Did you just read the same story I did? It really comes down to this: Do you trust that God is who he says he is? A God who will see you through to the other side? A God who has a plan and purpose for your life and is giving you ample opportunities to humbly submit to it and say *yes* to whatever it is that he's called you to?

To surrender control.

To take initiative.

To take the first step.

One final piece to the journey of Abraham. God not only redeems Abraham and Sarah by giving them a chance to start over, but he remembers Ishmael and sees Hagar.[33] He even says that Ishmael will be father to a great nation, which most historians agree came true.[34] God doesn't overlook anyone.

On That Very Day

I can't stop reading one phrase from Genesis 17:23: "On that very day." On that day, something clicked for Abraham. He trusted in who God claimed to be and he obeyed. He didn't wait, he jumped. That day, in Abraham's ninety-ninth year, was a catalyst on the trail God had called him to blaze. God said "jump" and Abraham leaped feet first into the unknown, blazing a trail for people as numerous as the stars to follow.[35]

I want you to take the leap, but I also want to make sure you're ready. Because if your character isn't up to the task, you're bound to fail. The foundation you depend on will fall apart. You'll end up like Abraham—trying to control the future your own way to receive the blessing you think you deserve. Your way (through worldly motivations) rather than the better one God wants to give you (heavenly motivations).

How can you ensure that *now* is the time to jump? Give some thought to the Three Rs.

- Repent
- Rebuild
- Release

Walk the Three Rs

God told Abraham to "walk before me faithfully and be blameless." In response, Abraham "fell facedown." Abraham responded in a posture of humility.

Do you have the self-awareness and the courage to look yourself in the mirror and ask God honestly, "Am I holding on to or hiding anything that I need to let go of?"

The word "to repent" is a translation of the Greek term *metanoia*. It literally means to "change your mind" or "turn around." It describes what happens when you decide that the way you're living hasn't worked and the time has come to return to the way of Jesus.

Be willing to go there. Do the hard work of bringing any unspoken sin into the light. The decreased weight on your back will serve you well for the trail to come.

Once you've repented and you believe you're ready to begin blazing the trail, rebuild an altar. Throughout Scripture we see altars used as physical reminders of the promises of God. Abraham's circumcision became his altar of remembrance for the promise God had given him.

Ask God for a clear reminder like this, to which you can return throughout your journey. When life gets hard, when you want to quit or give up, when bad things happen, what can remind you of why you began blazing the trail in the first place? What reminds you of the initial promise God made?

For me, it's a rock that I picked up in the middle of a prayer labyrinth (a longer story for another time). That rock is precious to me because it reminds me of the promise I felt God speak over me in that season of my life. It brings me back to the reasons why I'm seeking to blaze the trail God has set before me.

Once you believe that your character is in a right standing with God, and once you have something to mark the promise he's given you, then it's time to release. Seriously. It's time to *go*. Take the first step.

Now.

Remember Abraham? *On that very day*. If you're ready, God's ready.

Experience the Full Thrill

That day, I had to make a choice to step off that one-hundred-foot-tall platform. And you know what? I did.

I ended up riding the zip line four more times that weekend. I even started going backwards and contorting my body so I could look upside down.

How did I finally manage to experience the full thrill of that zipline? I overcame the initial fear it presented. I started seeing it, not as an obstacle in my way, but as an opportunity to grow. I had been offered the ride of a lifetime.

But I had to take it. No one could ride that zip line for me.

You're reading this, I presume, because you want to gain some insight into living the life of a Trailblazer. If so, that presupposes that God has placed a dream on your heart.

Think about it . . .

Keep thinking . . .

You got it?

Don't be ashamed of it. Don't be afraid of it. Don't allow insecurity or doubt to talk you off the ledge.

What's your God-given dream? Maybe it's to be a doctor, or a missionary in Taiwan, or a stay-at-home parent. If you had unlimited resources to go out and do _____, what would _____ be?

I won't let you off the hook on this one. Write it down right here:

MY DREAM:

_____

_____

_____

_____

_____

_____

_____

_____

Now, hang with me for a moment. Right now, you're on the edge, thinking that you're ready to jump into the abyss of the unknown to begin blazing the trail God's called you to. While God probably has you in a season of preparation leading up to this moment, let me be the first to say:

GO FOR IT! I believe in you.

Will you jump?

Will you take the first step?

The life of a Trailblazer is a life of initiative. It's time to say *yes* to the future God has waiting for you. If you're ready to blaze the trail, then take the first step and turn the page.

3

FAITHFULLY FIGHT INSECURITY

Submission

I DIDN'T THINK THIS BOOK would ever *really* be written.

I'm not posturing.

That's an honest assessment of where my faith stood prior to entering the world of authorship and publishing. To be completely transparent, I had *no* idea what I was getting myself into. I knew that God had called me to write. I knew that one day I wanted to be an author, to use words and sentences and paragraphs to move people from one point to another in their journey with Jesus.

But when I felt the Lord burden me with this dream in August 2020, I thought, *surely, there's no way he means now*.

But he did.

And that fall, I began a journey, one that continues now as I write, of learning what it means to live in a posture of submission.

A Volatile Relationship with Submission

My relationship with the character trait of submission has always been . . . well, volatile, to say the least.

I get it from my dad. Both of us oscillate between fearless faith and fearful control. And it's *exhausting*.

For instance, in 2001, my dad—at the time, a twenty-seven-year-old youth pastor–extraordinaire—packed up his wife, seven-year-old, and four-year-old into our car; put our stuff into a U-Haul; and with $5,000 in the bank, set out for Indianapolis, Indiana, to plant a church, "like no other before" (classic church-planter mentality).

We didn't know anyone there, hadn't seen the apartment we would occupy, and had no strategy for acquiring a place to gather and worship like, you know, one does in church. We lived with a dollar and a dream.

Bottom line: it was *crazy*.

And do you know what's crazier? It worked.

Our first gathering took place in our apartment complex clubhouse. Twelve people showed up, a dozen individuals who didn't know each other before that night. My dad cast vision like this: "Jesus had twelve disciples. Our church has twelve people. What can't God do?" (Again, major church-planter energy here.)

Within three years, the church ran five hundred people on any given Sunday. We were witnessing a modern-day miracle. Such is the "fearless faith" end of the spectrum in full swing.

Things were going well. *Really* well. We were living the dream. Submission to God's plan felt natural, anointed, blessed.

And then, doubts began to creep in. Questions arose within my father's heart. Somehow, he became convinced that it wasn't enough. Nothing was *ever* enough. He *never* felt satisfied. The seduction of success began to overtake him, which led him on a search for satisfaction anyplace he could find it. That search eventually led to an extramarital affair.[1]

In a three-day span, my dad obliterated his credibility, reputation, character, family, and community. In a fearful attempt to seize control, my dad lost everything he'd worked so hard to attain. It was a pattern his son (me) would end up repeating.

Now to be clear, I've had no extramarital affair, by the grace of God. But that oscillation between fearless faith and fearful control? It has upstarted and upended multiple moves of God in my life.

Surely, there's a better way to live than this, right, God?

Why am I always sabotaging myself?

Is there any way to drive out the fears, insecurities, and doubts attempting to overtake my mind and soul?

I finally found solace in the story of a man named Moses. His journey from fear to faith, from self-sabotage to submission, is one that we can and must learn from if we are to blaze the trail God's called us to.

Twists and Turns

From the onset, Moses' life overflowed with twists and turns. And yet, throughout his early years, we see a divine favor on Moses' life.

When Moses came on the scene, the Israelites, God's people, were slaves to the Egyptians. When Pharaoh decreed a nationwide genocide of Hebrew babies—trying to stem the tide of a growing foreign population—Moses got miraculously saved.[2]

How?

Fearless faith on the part of his mother.

Eventually, Moses murders a man, flees to the desert, and becomes a shepherd for forty years.[3]

And yet, God's sovereignty still overrules in Moses' life. This becomes apparent in Exodus 3.

Let's set the stage . . .

Moses has settled into his desert lifestyle. He's found a wife and been accepted into an incredible family, led by a wise father-in-law named Jethro. Moses' day job? Watch sheep. His night job? Watch more sheep.

It's a quiet life. A simple life. And Moses feels content.

One day, while tending sheep, Moses notices a bush on fire, but somehow it doesn't burn up. A curious sight! Curious enough for Moses to wander closer and see it for himself. And in Exodus 3, things start to heat up (bad dad joke; I'm sorry, it won't happen again):

> When the LORD saw that he had gone over to look, God called to him from within the bush, "Moses! Moses!"
> And Moses said, "Here I am."
> "Do not come any closer," God said. "Take off your sandals, for the place where you are standing is holy ground." Then he said, "I am the God of your father, the God of Abraham, the God of Isaac and the God of Jacob." At this, Moses hid his face, because he was afraid to look at God.
> The LORD said, "I have indeed seen the misery of my people in Egypt. I have heard them crying out because of their slave drivers, and I am concerned about their suffering."[4]

Now skip to verse 10: "So now, go. I am sending you to Pharaoh to bring my people the Israelites out of Egypt."

Talk about an introduction and an invitation!

Here we see a theme that reappears time and again throughout Scripture. God tells his people "go" and expects a faith-filled response of obedience. We saw it with Abraham, we see it here with Moses, and we'll see it again with other Trailblazers.

"Go. I'm sending you to Pharaoh."

Can you imagine? Being told that you must face your most intimidating enemy? Getting sent back to the place of your darkest shame, your worst sin, your deepest fear, and your biggest regret? Why, God, would you call Moses to return to the one place he never wanted to see again?

Have you ever found yourself asking a similar question?

"Why, God, do you want me to try to have children again after three miscarriages?"

"Why, God, do you want me to try marriage again when I've been cheated on twice?"

"Why, God, do you want me to start that business when I embarrassingly filed for bankruptcy a decade earlier?"

"Why, God, do you want me to face and forgive my abuser?"

"Why, God, do you want me to start this endeavor when all I heard growing up was that I'd never amount to anything?"

Why, God?

God's invitations have a way of evoking our deepest fears and insecurities. God desires to meet us in the muck and mess of our souls and to heal us, to grow us, and to push us toward a better and more whole version of ourselves.

But it's not easy. In fact, it's anything *but* easy. And the fleshly motivators will come out of the woodwork to convince you that you should just give up. Look at how Moses' insecurity began to take over the conversation: "But Moses said to God, 'Who am I that I should go to Pharaoh and bring the Israelites out of Egypt?'"[5]

Insecurity immediately began to rear its ugly head. How often have you found yourself in a position to do something great, when insecurity started to pull you away?

"*You*? You really think *you* can do that?"

"I'm not sure if I'm the right person for the job."

"I doubt I have what it takes."

"I lack the skills that he/she possesses."

"I'm not _____ enough."

Insecurity is a gigantically toxic motivator because it holds the power to tear us down and take us apart before we even begin blazing the trail God's set out for us.

In a flash, Moses convinced himself that everything God had said was a lie because he was a fraud.

Feel familiar?

God calls us worthy, but we tell ourselves we're worthless. Or God calls us to a particular job, location, or person, but we think, *I don't think I have what it takes.* It's as insidious to God now as it was when Moses said it thousands of years ago.

Insecurity is a slippery slope. As soon as we begin telling ourselves lies, we run the risk of believing them. This is where the doubt comes in. Consider Moses' response: "Suppose I go to the Israelites and say to them, 'The God of your fathers has sent me to you,' and they ask me, 'What is his name?' Then what shall I tell them?"[6]

God had announced his presence through a burning bush. Yes, that's as crazy as it sounds. And yet, Moses had the audacity to ask, "Oh, by the way, let's theoretically say I do what you're asking; what would I even tell them? Who are you?"

Doubt had begun to creep in.

"God, you keep telling me you'll be with me, but I don't even know if I believe you. Who are you?"

God complied and told Moses, "I AM WHO I AM. This is what you are to say to the Israelites: 'I AM has sent me to you.'"[7] Moses' questions left God undeterred. In the very next verse, God tells Moses to assemble the elders and to proclaim that he'd been sent to liberate the Israelites from slavery. You know, a very casual ask.

Moses' doubt really dug in at this point and more questions came: "What if they don't believe me?" "What if they don't listen?" "What if they doubt?"

God then performed a few miraculous signs before Moses, further indicating that he could be trusted.[8] But Moses' doubts continued. He declared his inability to speak eloquently and assured God that this handicap disqualified him from the task. God grew angry and further encouraged Moses to trust him.

This is the problem with insecurity and doubt: it becomes a slippery slope. If you're not careful, your insecurity will lead to doubt, which will end in despair.

Notice how after multiple exhortations, signs and wonders, and an *amazing* confirmation from the God of the universe himself, Moses dejectedly replies, "Pardon your servant, Lord. Please send someone else."[9]

I wonder how many incredible things individuals *haven't* accomplished because they could never overcome their internal dialogue of insecurity, doubt, and despair?

The life you've always wanted lies before you. What God has called you to, he will see you through. But you must believe and submit to the calling he's placed on your life.

I've experienced and I sympathize with being degraded, put down, and doubted by others. It's not fun. But I believe we often miss out on blazing the trail God's called us to because of self-sabotage. We don't trust that God can do through us what we believe he's said he'll do through us.

Moses must make a choice.

Will he go and obey God? Or will he continue to sulk in his sin, wallow in his past, and miss out on becoming the vessel through whom God would rescue an entire nation?

Trade in Fear for Faith

Similarly, we must choose. Trailblazers live in a posture of submission. To blaze trails never before traversed takes courage, discipline, and devotion (all qualities we'll later discuss in further detail). Without a posture of submission, however, we'll never get on the trail in the first place.

What will you choose? The way of Jesus or the dungeon of doubt?

Submission to God doesn't mean an absence of trials on the road ahead, but it does secure his presence on the journey. To practice submission is to trade in fear for faith. Or in other words, to be a Trailblazer means to consistently choose faith over fear. Which will it be?

The interaction between Moses and God shows us that although we have the gift of free will, God's "go" will always outweigh our "no." This doesn't mean that we'll always choose God's way but that his way will always lead to better, greater, or holier things.

Many equate having "faith" with being "fearless." They say that to have faith is to have no fear. But that's *not* the biblical narrative. Just consider Jesus. In the garden of Gethsemane, Jesus knelt to pray, "sorrowful and troubled."[10] He cried out, "My Father, if it is possible, may this cup be taken from me. Yet not as I will, but as you will."[11]

That sounds less "fearless" to me than it does "submissive."

Jesus, despite his desire to avoid dying on a cross, prays, "not as

I will, but as you will." Submission doesn't usher away fear. Rather, submission ushers in trust despite the fear that persists.

I love how one of my favorite songwriters puts it. He says, "I've learnt faith isn't fearless. It's just trusting when you fear the most."[12]

That is submission.

That's choosing faith over fear.

And *that* is the way of the Trailblazer.

The sooner we say yes to God's call, the sooner we can enter the blessing of what God has promised us. We can experience life to the full *if* we'll submit to Jesus' trail of character formation.

Will it be easy? No. But it will be worth it.

I know from experience what it looks like to wander from God's call . . . and to suffer for it.

Anything but Ministry

As I entered college, I did so fully expecting that I'd enter the health industry. My parents' story, while a beautiful tale of redemption and restoration (which we'll consider later), had turned me off to the church. I distrusted pastors and clergy, cynically believing they all were hiding something. But neither did I trust people who attended church, because I had seen, heard, and witnessed—firsthand—the vitriol, backlash, and venom thrust upon my dad and our family for his sinful actions.

I'll be the first to say that my dad's extramarital affair was wrong. I believe his actions merited just consequences. But *no one* can stray too far from the grace of Jesus Christ. No one! Some at our church said otherwise and the church cast us out. Even to this day, some of those relationships remain broken.

All of this prompted me to have nothing to do with ministry. I describe my freshman year of college as The Boring Prodigal

Son[13] story. I, like the Prodigal Son of Scripture, essentially ran away from home. My newfound independence and anonymity provided me with the requisite space to run from everything that I knew, believed, and trusted about God. For a season, I basically gave up on my faith. I didn't start drinking, taking drugs, or hiring prostitutes, but I did fling myself into a whole lot of animosity and aloofness.

Until March 16, 2016.

For the first time in months, I felt a tug on my heart to open my Bible. After an awkward conversation with what others might have considered an invisible friend, I moseyed over to my backpack and pulled out the Bible I used for class (health major, but still attending Bible school). Passive aggressively, I mumbled under my breath, "Speak, God."

To be clear, this is not and never will be the best way to hear from God. I lacked an attitude or heart posture of openness or invitation. I'd closed myself off to the presence of God. I'd simply run out of ideas.

And yet, even in my stubbornness, God wanted to speak to me. Without expecting much, I initiated what I dubbed "the holy drop." Have you heard of it? It goes like this: open your Bible, drop it on a hard surface, and see to what passage it opens (do *not* practice this at home!).

Terrible, terrible strategy.

Nonetheless, I did it. And lo and behold, my Bible opened to Exodus 3—the story we just read, Moses and the burning bush.

About an hour later, I found myself flat on my face, weeping, pleading with God to send someone else. In that moment, I recognized that I also was in the desert. I also was in exile. I had been wallowing in my sin, shame, hurt, and pain.

And that day, God called me. He reminded me of who he is, of who I am, and of what he had put me on this earth to do.

After delivering every excuse possible, I surrendered my life to Jesus and committed to serving him for the rest of my days. And man, do I wish that I could sign, "happily ever after" here and refund the rest of your money! But that's not how the journey with Christ goes.

That night I surrendered to blazing a trail. But following Jesus requires *daily* surrender, *daily* submission, year in and year out. At every turn, the life-altering question will confront us: Faith or fear? Every time that I've submitted to fear-less-than (not fearless) faith, rather than fear-filled control, I've seen moves of God unlike anything I can describe.

This book, in and of itself, provides one such piece of evidence.

Do Nazirites Write Books?

Numbers 6 introduces us to "the Nazirite Vow."[14] Feel free to read for yourself, but basically a Nazirite would make a vow of consecration (the act of being set apart), which included a vow of abstinence. Nazirites would abstain from touching the dead, from drinking alcohol, and from cutting their hair.

In August of 2020, I came to believe—through an encouraging and prophetic conversation with a friend—that the Lord had asked me to take the message of Trailblazers further than I ever had dreamed. I felt pressed to write a book.

My only problem: I had no idea how to write a book.

And so, I decided to make a Nazirite Vow, believing that God would fulfill his promise as I lived in submission to him. For seventeen months, I didn't cut my hair. I performed no funerals. And I didn't drink alcohol. I sensed God forming and shaping my character, growing in me a firm resolve to submit to him, whatever the cost.

At the end of that seventeen months, I looked like a homeless person masquerading as a pastor. My hair had begun to grow split ends, my beard stretched far longer than my wife's taste preferred, and quite honestly, I didn't love how I looked. Almost every day, insecurity, doubt, and the threat of despair crept in.

Is this really something I should be doing, God?

Who am I to ever write a book?

I don't know the first thing about this process.

God, what if I fail?

But the promise remained: "What I have seen you to, I will see you through. Will you trust me? Will you trust that I Am who I say I Am?"

Living into this promise has generated more fear than perhaps anything else in my life. Writing a book forces you to bare your soul. I will have left nothing unturned in my heart by the time you get to the final page. But God continues to teach me that our job isn't to succeed but to submit and allow him to sustain. I'm telling the truth when I say that I didn't think this book would ever be written.

Deep down, though, I held onto the belief that God would create an opportunity for me to share this story. Still, I had no idea it would turn into an actual, published book.

And yet, here we are.

Submission to the gracious God of wonders grants us unexpected invitations to experience wonder ourselves.

Your Will Be Done

So, what about you? What's God calling you to?

Does your call scare you? Good! Because if it doesn't, it's too safe.

And if it does scare you, then know that God extends an invitation to you to trust him despite the presence of your fear, to have faith that God has a good plan designed specifically for you. The trail he's called you to blaze will come equipped with everything you need to lead the way.

Begin the practice of submission today. If you have no idea where to begin, let me suggest the Lord's Prayer as a great place to start.

I love Jesus' line, "your kingdom come, your will be done, on earth as it is in heaven."[15] That, my friend, is a prayer of submission.

Pray that prayer daily and see what God begins to do in your heart and in your life.

As you work on and sharpen the practice of submission, watch and witness as God begins to shape and form you into the person he always destined you to become.

4

DEVOTED AT THE RIGHT COST

Loyalty

AS I WRITE, A WAR RAGES IN UKRAINE. Russia's president, Vladimir Putin, wants to reclaim the sovereign country of Ukraine in an attempt to reform and reshape a modern-day version of the Soviet Union. It breaks my heart to see these events unfold. To date, thousands of Ukrainians have been killed, including hundreds of children, with many more injured or displaced.[1]

Despite the tragic events and senseless casualties taking place, the world has fixed its eyes on Ukraine's president, Volodymyr Zelensky. Despite constant pressure from the United States and other Western countries to flee the country for his own safety and for the preservation of government order, Zelensky has repeatedly refused.

His reason?

"We are here. We are in Kyiv. We are protecting Ukraine."[2]

This quote came on day 2 of Russia's invasion, alongside four high-level Ukrainian government officials. They spoke in the streets of the capital, at the very time when Russian forces were closing in on the city. The strength and fortitude of these leaders had captured the world's hearts.

"What courage, what strength, what unity!" I've heard some say.

But underneath all those truthful descriptors lies a character quality that no one can instantaneously generate.

Loyalty.

It's a trait inherited either by culture or nurture. We gain the trait of loyalty either by learning it or by developing it. In the case of Zelensky—considering Ukraine's history and what's known as a "strong group"[3] culture—his loyalty came both through learning and developing.

With his country at war, his people endangered, and destruction looming on all sides, Zelensky's loyalty to his people and his country have reminded the world how critical the possession of such a trait is in the life of a Trailblazer.

Loyalty has a way of overriding previous opinions, conclusions, and outlooks regarding individuals and legacies. Think about it: prior to becoming the leader of the greatest nonviolent resistance ever seen, Mahatma Gandhi worked as a lawyer from Gujarat.[4]

Michael Jordan, prior to earning his reputation as the best basketball player to ever live, was a scrawny kid from Wilmington, North Carolina, whose coach had cut him in his sophomore year from the varsity basketball team.[5]

Tom Hanks, before becoming one of the world's most famous movie stars, was a social outcast. As he puts it, "I was a geek, a spaz. I was horribly, painfully, terribly shy."[6]

None of these three men would be known for their exploits today if not for an intense devotion and loyalty to their craft or calling.

History typically remembers only those with the strongest of convictions, who remain loyal to a fault, for better or for worse.

Zelensky is a comedian-turned-president. He turned a 2015 TV show (in which he starred) into a presidential campaign slogan.[7] But history will always remember the moment Ukraine's president stepped out into the battle and rallied his people by declaring his devotion and loyalty in the face of intense threat and opposition.

Loyalty leaves a legacy.

Loyalty has the power to transform reputations.

Where does someone's loyalty lie when their back is against the wall? The answer to that question usually defines their future. Such is the case for our next hero of the faith, a lowly prostitute-turned-saint, transformed through the supernatural loyalty she demonstrated.

I'd like to introduce you to Rahab.

A Prostitute's Motivation

Rahab's story takes place against the backdrop of an Israelite leadership transition. Moses had handed over the reins to his apprentice, Joshua. Joshua would lead Israel in its efforts to claim the Promised Land that God told Abraham his descendants would one day inhabit.

In preparation for the war to come, Joshua shrewdly sent two spies to scope out their enemy. The two spies enter Jericho, a desirable coastal city with fertile farming lands around it and an array of natural resources at its disposal.

Their first stop? The house of a prostitute named Rahab.[8]

Whaaat? Let me explain.

Scholars have provided two explanations for why the Israelite spies might have chosen to post up at Rahab's place:

- To secure Rahab's services (though the character they show throughout their interaction leads away from this conclusion).

- As a strategic hideout, knowing that a prostitute's house would provide a revolving door of strangers looking to remain under the radar as they engaged in illicit acts.

I think it makes sense to believe the two spies differed from the other . . . er, visitors . . . to the house. Therefore, I choose to believe the latter, but you can make your own conclusion.

That night, informants alerted the king of Jericho to the presence of Israelite spies.[9] I believe that the spies' countercultural treatment of this woman tipped off someone looking to make a quick buck. The king sent word to Rahab to turn over the spies to him, but something strange ends up happening. Rather than turning the spies over to the king, Rahab hides them. And then, it gets even crazier.

Rahab concocts an elaborate lie that sends the king's soldiers searching for the spies on the outskirts of the city, even while the spies continue to hang out with Rahab. She had hidden them on her roof.[10]

Here we have a pagan prostitute, from a foreign land, harboring spies of an enemy nation intent on scoping out a way to obliterate her people, take captive her city, and change the world as she knows it.

Now are you confused?

Why would Rahab do this? Does she have some vendetta against the king? Perhaps a sordid history between them? Does Rahab have her own agenda? Does she wish to see the deconstruction of her government and people? Or is something else going on here? We finally get some clarity in Joshua 2, beginning in verse 8:

> I know that the LORD has given you this land and that a great fear of you has fallen on us, so that all who live in this country are melting in fear because of you. We have heard how the LORD dried up the water of the Red Sea for you when you came out of Egypt, and what you did to Sihon

and Og, the two kings of the Amorites east of the Jordan, whom you completely destroyed. When we heard of it, our hearts melted in fear and everyone's courage failed because of you, for the LORD your God is God in heaven above and on the earth below.[11]

Whoa. Talk about a curveball! But this reveals a moment.

Here, with her back against the wall, we see where Rahab's loyalty lies. When the king of Jericho breathes down her neck, demanding that she surrender the harbored spies, what does she do? She disobeys. She fabricates a story to try to keep safe the presumed enemy.

Now, why would she do that? The answer seems simple: loyalty.

Here we witness Rahab pledge her allegiance to the "God in heaven above and on the earth below." This becomes a legacy-defining moment, where we see the proverbial "fork in the road" placed in front of Rahab. She must choose.

So, too, must *you* choose. Will you play it safe or blaze the trail?

Somehow, someway, God had revealed to this pagan prostitute that he had made her for *more*. That her worth didn't rest in her occupation. That her future didn't depend on the actions of a (presumably) immoral king. No. Rahab had a choice to pledge her loyalty and allegiance, in faith, to the God of the Israelites.

As a result, the spies sneak away without harm. The Israelites then destroy Jericho, while sparing Rahab and her family.[12] Rather than dying as just another pagan prostitute, Rahab and company get adopted into the family of Israel, a decision that changes the trajectory and legacy of her life forever.

You may say, "Cool story, Micah. But . . . so what? What's this have to do with me?"

Simple: You're a Trailblazer, right? Or at least, you want to be. If so, then you, too, must choose where your loyalty lies.

Will you allow the labels placed on you by others, by society, or by your mistakes to define you? Or will you, at this moment, choose to chart a different course and blaze a different trail?

I write these words believing that you may have picked up this book even though a voice persists in lying to you, saying, "God could never use me because of what I've done." If that's the case, then know that I've written this for *you*.

That is the motivator of shame at play. This nagging feeling that you *are* what you've *done*. That your worst moment makes you *the worst*. That your most embarrassing moment makes *you* an embarrassment. That your biggest failure makes *you* a failure.

Do you see shame at work in your life? Have you succumbed again and again to this false belief that your past will always define your present and future? If that describes you, then with as much passion as I can possibly muster, hear me:

It's.

Not.

True!

You are *not* your mistakes. You are *not* your deepest regrets. You are *not* the sum total of your shame.

Jesus, through his sacrifice on the cross, took on the weight of all of that and by the power of his blood, healed you. Today, you have an opportunity to believe that your story can change. That as a redeemed, chosen, anointed individual, God himself has gifted you an opportunity to live life to the full.

But again, I insist: *you must choose*. Loyalty to a lie or loyalty to the Lord of Lords?

The life of a Trailblazer waits for you, at a cost.

But it's a price worth paying.

Is the Cost Worth the Price?

Our loyalty to Jesus *will* cost us. There's really no way around it. Jesus clearly says, "Those of you who do not give up everything you have cannot be my disciples."[13] So, is the cost worth the price? Is the price of obedience worth the shedding of your shame?

I believe so. When we pledge our loyalty to Jesus, we effectively surrender some things that the world deems valuable:

Money.

Possessions.

Fantasies.

Power.

The list goes on . . .

But we gain an ability to live life authentically, true to who we are: broken human beings seeking to fulfill God's will, which means establishing his Kingdom on earth as it is in heaven.

We become people of love, joy, peace, patience, kindness, goodness, gentleness, and self-control.[14]

Is such a life really possible? Yes! Consider a few ways to begin blazing the trail God has for you.

1. Press into your weaknesses as evidence of God's strength.

Rahab's response to the spies always catches me off guard. I mean, if I were Rahab, I would have replied something like, "Hi, yes, I know what my house looks like. But this isn't a brothel. What those men are saying about me is not true. I'm not like that. I gave up all of that. I'm a good person. Would you please have mercy on me when you attack my city?"

And yet, we hear no hint of shame in Rahab's response. I don't acknowledge this fact to justify Rahab's occupation but simply to point out that Rahab focused more on God's strength than on her weakness. Rather than trying to save face and earn favor with the spies, she simply acknowledged who God is, what he can do, and that she'd surrendered to him.

What if we took on the same posture? What if we stopped pretending to be better than we really are? What if we stopped hiding behind social media feeds and Snapchat filters, trying to win or earn approval from others? What if, instead, we acknowledged that Jesus is Lord and believed Paul's words: "When I am weak, then I am strong"?[15]

We find no heroes in this story other than God. Rahab didn't give Israel the victory. Neither did the spies. God and God alone won the war. But God chose to use a prostitute to blaze the trail for Israel to step further into God's will for his chosen people.

As we press into our weaknesses, we highlight God's strength. Our tragedies in life become testimonies of God's all-conquering power, love, and mercy.

Stop running from shame! Instead, press into your story. When you do, watch how God uses your weakness as evidence of his strength.

2. By faith, obey.

I can't imagine what it'd feel like for the most powerful person in my country of origin to pressure me into doing something I didn't want to do. And yet, that's just where Rahab found herself. She sat on the king's hot seat to give up these spies.

Yet, Rahab refused.

By faith, she obeyed what she sensed the Lord had asked her to do.

How often do we act with that same posture? No president has ever pressured me, but I've certainly felt tempted to down red Solo cups in high school, sleep with my girlfriend before marriage, cheat on my taxes, look at pornography, and steal items that belonged to someone else (among other things).

In every one of those situations, the same question has arisen: Micah, will you obey the world or obey God? Or another (better, I believe) way to put it: Will you trust yourself, Micah, or will you trust God?

Author Pete Greig summarizes the act of following Jesus like this: "Listen and obey."[16] Could it really be that simple?

If we don't believe God is who he says he is, then living a life of faithful obedience will become tragically difficult for us. We must choose. Will we compromise or uphold the way of Jesus?

To live in faithful obedience means to refuse to compromise, even if others around us cave left and right. To live in faithful obedience means not to compromise, even if other *Christians* do. Faithful obedience means staying true to who God has called us to be and what God has called us to, even if it's not the "popular" decision.

Think about it: Rahab housing these spies could've gotten her killed. Yet by faith and in obedience, she did what she believed God had called her to do. Her choice saved her life.

Will you become an individual who drives out shame and faithfully obeys the calling God has placed on your life? If so, a trail awaits to be blazed that could alter your future forever.

3. Graciously accept the invitation of transformation.

Gandhi, Michael Jordan, Tom Hanks—none of these men ever would have achieved recognition without a deep commitment to inward and outward transformation.

Gandhi committed to practicing nonviolence.

Michael Jordan committed to honing his basketball skills.

Tom Hanks committed to getting out of his comfort zone and sharpening his acting chops.

They all understood that to become the best required intense devotion over a long stretch of time. Their loyalty outlasted every other person in their field.

Why don't we treat our apprenticeship to Jesus the same way? I love how Eugene Peterson describes a life following Jesus: "A long obedience in the same direction."[17] *That's* our call.

Press Into, Press Beyond

Day in and day out, we press into who Jesus is while we press beyond the lie and motivator of shame that seeks to hold us down and hold us back.

Between us and the person Jesus longs for us to become lies a chasm of the unknown. In its depths lurk fear, worry, anxiety, and doubt. On the other side of that chasm, however, beckons a life of faith, hope, love, joy, peace, patience, kindness, goodness, faithfulness, gentleness, and self-control. It's possible to reach the other side!

But you must be willing to say yes to the trail that God's called you to blaze. And then you must develop the fortitude to stay on it and to remain loyal, even when times get hard.

A life of spiritual formation is no efficient, overnight-success, immediate-payoff process. It's slow, quiet, and mundane. Day by day, however, as you commit to a long obedience in the same direction—slowly but surely—the gift of retrospect grows clear.

Just as Rahab could look back at a past of prostitution and look ahead toward a future of freedom, we, too, can look back at a life of shame and then forward to a future of salvation in Christ Jesus. In his kindness, God often uses our deepest hurts and regrets as the foundation for our greatest contributions to the redemptive story of God. All of us can discover redemption in retrospect. Rahab's story provides an amazing case in point.

Matthew introduces us to the genealogy of Jesus in the first chapter of his Gospel. Before Matthew ever describes the life of Jesus, he invites us to reminisce on how Jesus came to be. And he shows us how miraculously and graciously God chose to use ordinary people as conduits for the arrival of the Savior of the world.

Interlaced throughout Matthew's genealogy are Trailblazers, some we've covered (Abraham) and others we'll soon get to (David). Yet, tucked deep into the family tree is a curious pair: "Salmon the father of Boaz, whose mother was Rahab, Boaz the father of Obed, whose mother was Ruth, Obed the father of Jesse, and Jesse the father of King David."[18]

When Rahab said yes to allegiance to God, she didn't save only her family from certain destruction, or merely ensure a new life and a new future for herself. In fact, Rahab's yes signaled her acceptance of an invitation to play a key part in the redemptive story of God. She not only helped bring about God's will for his chosen people but helped to usher in the Savior of the world.

In the moment, we often don't realize the impact of our faithful obedience. Yet, when we have a minute to recollect the important moments of our lives, we usually find God's kindness and mercy extended toward us in abundance. Our obedience often puts us on a trail that leaves a *far* bigger impact than we could ever imagine.

A Loyalty Unmatched

A few years ago, I found myself engaging in an exercise called the genogram,[19] a discipleship tool used to chart your family history to uncover any relational strongholds or generational sins. It offers the hope that in discovering the toxic aspects of your family of origin, you can begin an intentional journey of healing as you seek to break those strongholds.

I'll never forget charting my own genogram.

Not only did I have to wade through my dad's story of infidelity, but as I worked my way down my family tree, I discovered that *many* members of my family had gotten mired in infidelity and divorce. In fact, roughly 80 percent of my mom and dad's extended family— dating back to my great, great grandparents—had *at least* one failed marriage. In other words, my parents had the odds stacked against them. So, when my dad committed adultery, one could've seen it as yet another tragic event in a family marred by the generational sin of unfaithfulness.

But that wasn't the end of this story.

In humble obedience to God, my mom mustered up the courage to forgive my father. And in humble obedience to God, my dad authentically repented and turned away from a life of hiding, a life dominated by shame.

Over the course of three months (and in some ways, the last eighteen years and counting), my parents chose to submit to God rather than to the way of the world. Rather than taking the easier and justified route of divorce, my mother remained committed to the vows she spoke on her wedding day. Rather than taking the easier route of hiding, deflecting, and running, my dad bravely faced, head on, the mistakes, sins, and disease within his soul.

By pledging their loyalty to God and by faithfully obeying his commands to repent and forgive, my parents began blazing a new trail that will have ripple effects for generations to come. Because of their commitment to restoration, a new path formed in our family tree. Rather than becoming yet another statistic, my parents modeled for my siblings and me what true commitment looks like.

Not only has my life and marriage been forever changed because of their story, but my kids, grandkids, and on down the line will be able to look back to the marriage that could've and should've ended like all the rest . . . but yet persevered to the end.

A loyalty unmatched.

The promise-keeping power of God overshadowed Rahab's occupation of "prostitute."

The awesome grace of Jesus overcame my father's label of "adulterer."

And the sweet mercy of Christ Jesus can overcome whatever shame holds *you* back from stepping onto the trail that God has called you to blaze.

This is the power of loyalty.

When we devote ourselves to God, when we pledge our allegiance to Jesus before all other things, shame loses its hold on us. And so, day by day, in a long obedience in the same direction, we can grow into the Trailblazer God always meant us to be.

LEARN TO BE ALONE

Solitude

"GOD, WHAT ARE YOU DOING?"

Those words never came out of my mouth, but I might as well have been screaming them at the top of my lungs in my soul.

I was visiting one of my favorite places in the entire world, a prayer labyrinth in the middle of a spiritual retreat center that I frequent.[1] That prayer labyrinth and I have gone ten rounds together over the years. I've brought some of my deepest cries and most exciting celebrations before the Lord here. It's sacred ground.

"God, what are you doing?"

I found myself in this place of intense grief, feeling spiritually attacked on every side. I had no idea what to do other than to work it out in the prayer labyrinth. I knew that in the middle of such inner turmoil, my only way out was solitude.

But it wasn't always this way . . .

Drowning in Noise

My junior year of high school etched a memory in my mind of just how unhealthy I had become, drowning myself in the constant noise of everyday life. During my junior year, my on-again, off-again girlfriend and I broke up.

Hopeless romantic that I am, I felt crushed.

Rejection, insecurity, and a deep sadness began to rise to the surface. I hadn't performed on the basketball court as I'd hoped, either. In fact, I found myself in and out of the varsity rotation when I had fully expected to contribute in a big way.

Image conscious ⇨ image crushed.

Performance driven ⇨ performance failed.

Am I being melodramatic? Sure. But teenage angst gives me a pass, right? I saw my whole world coming to an end. In fact, I had ventured into some of the deepest unhealth someone wired like me (introverted, Enneagram 3) could experience.

Today, I see it as my first real face-to-face encounter with adversity. Sure, I had faced adversity before; but this time, I felt all on my own. I really was, in some ways; and in this instance, that was a good thing. As a seventeen-year-old growing into an adult, I needed to face myself in the mirror.

Who am I without a girlfriend?

Who am I without basketball?

Who am I when things go south?

Who am I when I've lost everything that gives me status, worth, and acceptance?

Hard questions at a time that demanded real answers!

But instead of facing my deepest fears and insecurities, I hid.

No, I ran.

Actually, I hid *and* ran.

I allowed the noise to overcome me and then drowned myself in escape. Incessant use of social media, binge-watching YouTube, pirated movies,[2] dipping my toes into pornography, serial dating, long drives blasting music, or initiating and engaging in conversations solely through a screen—my life had become one big distraction. One large escape.

A life full of noise.

I had lost touch with my ability to be alone.

I'd fallen into a habit of escaping to parties after basketball games so that I wouldn't have to go home and think about how well I did (or didn't) play. I also knew I wouldn't have to be alone there. At those parties was alcohol.

Pass. *I'm an underaged pastor's kid; I don't drink alcohol.*

At least some conscience still lived down there.

But those parties also featured girls. Girls who gave the affirmation and adoration I so desperately craved. And so, I'd move from one girl to another, until they felt comfortable enough to kiss me. Your average teenaged playboy.

I promise you I feel more sickened than you do.

It all came to a head one early December night. Going full mack mode, I found myself an hour into a party already having kissed three girls. The hedonistic pushback may be, "What's the big deal, Micah? It's not like you were sleeping with all these women!" That's true. But I nonetheless used those girls for my own personal pleasure—and for that, I remain deeply repentant.

Something about this night felt *different*. For the first time in a long while, I felt myself seeing life unfolding before me from the prover-bial perspective of a fly on the wall.

I saw *myself*: an insecure, broken, fearful, lost young man trying so hard to be loved.

And for the first time, I had compassion on myself. I felt genuinely sorry for what I had done and who I had become. And so, I did the only thing I knew to do. I called my dad.

"Hello?"

"Dad, it's me."

"What's up, man? It's late. Are you okay?"

"Yeah, Dad, I'm fine. I just need you to know that I kissed three girls tonight and I feel so gross, so dirty, and so ashamed."

A long silence.

"Thanks for telling me. I love you and I'm with you. Do me a favor?"

"Yeah, Dad, anything."

"Go apologize to those girls, and then go outside and I want you to just take a walk and spend some time with the Lord."

"Okay, Dad."[3]

I hung up, found those three girls, and told them I was sorry for taking advantage of them. And then I walked out of that house and into the night . . . by myself.

A Trail of Solitude

If we should look at any person as a Trailblazer in the realm of solitude, it's King David. The Psalms give us a master class in conversing with the soul. Beautiful and mystifying experiences often occur in the context of solitude.[4]

From the onset, David lays out the importance of solitude. Look in Psalm 1, beginning in verse 1:

> Blessed is the one
>   who does not walk in step with the wicked
> or stand in the way that sinners take
>   or sit in the company of mockers,
> but whose delight is in the law of the LORD,
>   and who meditates on his law day and night.
> That person is like a tree planted by streams of water,
>   which yields its fruit in season
> and whose leaf does not wither—
>   whatever they do prospers.[5]

The first three verses of the Psalm awaken us to the reality that, "[he] who meditates on [God's] law day and night . . . is like a tree planted by streams of water." What a beautiful picture of solitude's potential!

Do we not feel the weight of this?

We live in a world of overstimulation. Of constant noise. Of mind-numbing inundation. This noise pokes and prods at us day and night, seeking to steal our peace with the world's anxious agendas.

Have we ever stopped to ask ourselves why? Why the wheel never stops turning? Why the lights never shut off? Why the hum of the day only slows and never slumbers?

Could it be that we deeply fear what silence may bring? Does the thought of being alone overwhelm us with dread?

Silence and solitude make us vulnerable. To be silent, still, and alone before God is to uncover and unmask whatever muck and filth we've accumulated from the world and to present ourselves honestly and openly before the Lord. In that context we bring and lay down all our emotions, whether praises, celebrations, insecurities, doubts, or fears.

The opening lines of Psalms 8, 9, and 10 suggest for us a few of the many emotions David brought before the Lord in solitude.

> LORD, our Lord,
>   how majestic is your name in all the earth!
> You have set your glory
>   in the heavens.[6]

> I will give thanks to you, LORD, with all my heart;
>   I will tell of all your wonderful deeds.
> I will be glad and rejoice in you;
>   I will sing the praises of your name, O Most High.[7]

> Why, LORD, do you stand far off?
>   Why do you hide yourself in times of trouble?[8]

Perhaps that last line makes you a tad uncomfortable. Are we *allowed* to talk to God like that?

According to David, yes. Because solitude is the safe place, the place where we can bare our souls—naked and unashamed—and commune with the Father. In that space our desire intertwines with his, leaving us feeling more seen, known, and loved.

In solitude we also find answers. Because we often read the Psalms continuously, we tend to believe David wrote them continuously, as if all these revelations came to his mind at once. But that's not how writing works. Even as I write, I've stopped, taken breaks, reverted, revised, and redacted.

If only the writing of words could be as smooth as reading them!

But Psalm 15 takes issue with any such idea. There we see one example of David seeking answers in the quiet place and giving his soul time to receive from the Lord: "LORD, who may dwell in your sacred tent? Who may live on your holy mountain?"[9]

David asks the question and then seems to answer it on behalf of the Lord. Did he receive immediate revelation? I doubt it. I believe

David asked the question and then waited for the Lord to speak. Perhaps minutes, hours, or even days elapsed before verses 2 to 5 came to be.

An answer eventually came to David's quiet, centered heart. In the quiet place, solitude, we can find answers to our questions.[10] In solitude we also find rest for our weary souls.

With the constant barrage of noise beating and berating us, our soul longs for reprieve. We long to feel rested, energized, and filled. But where and how can such a refilling happen? I believe it can take place in the sacred, safe space of solitude.

King David alludes to this in perhaps his most well-known Psalm:

> The LORD is my shepherd, *I lack nothing*.
>   He makes me lie down in green pastures,
> he *leads me beside quiet waters*,
>   he *refreshes my soul*.
> He guides me along the right paths
>   for his name's sake.
> Even though I walk
>   through the darkest valley,
> I will fear no evil,
>   for you are with me;
> your rod and your staff,
>   they comfort me.
>
> You prepare a table before me
>   in the presence of my enemies.
> You anoint my head with oil;
>   *my cup overflows*.
> Surely your goodness and love will follow me
>   all the days of my life,
> and I will dwell in the house of the LORD
>   forever.[11]

Although many of us know this passage of Scripture, I wonder how many of us take advantage of the blueprint that David provides for us? One of my heroes[12] puts it more bluntly in his paraphrase: "True to your word, you let me catch my breath."[13]

My friend, do you need to catch your breath?

Has the never-ending noisiness of life drowned out your true self?

When you look in the mirror, do you know who stares back at you? If not, then Jesus has an invitation for you. Here's Eugene Peterson again, now paraphrasing the words of Jesus: "Are you tired? Worn out? Burned out on religion? Come to me. *Get away with me* and you'll recover your life. I'll show you how to take a *real rest*. Walk with me and work with me—*watch how I do it*. Learn the *unforced rhythms of grace*. I won't lay anything heavy or ill-fitting on you. Keep company with me and you'll learn to live freely and lightly."[14]

Does your soul leap at such an invitation? If so, perhaps the time has come to begin blazing a trail of solitude in your life. Such solitude kept David sane in the most difficult moments of life. It kept him humble in his most humiliating moments. And it provided a space to freely worship, celebrate, and honor God in his best moments.

Has noise driven you to the edge? If so, come back to Jesus. Take a real rest. Get alone with God. And allow him to blaze new trails in your soul, trails that will become springs of living water, allowing you to become who God created you to be.

Solitude provides space for us to be vulnerable, ask questions, receive answers, and enter true rest. But only the bold—those willing to face their true selves—end up reaping the benefits of this practice. Solitude delivers a centered spirit impossible to replicate outside of the crucible of quiet.

Will you blaze the trail?

Give Him the Space to Speak

As I walked away from that long-ago party, the dark night before me felt darker than usual. I felt as though I were walking into literal and figurative darkness, all at once. Darkness consumed me and I didn't know when the light would show itself.

I started walking and kept walking for what felt like the whole night (but was probably only thirty minutes). I had no destination in mind; I just hoped to escape the noise of that night. Eventually, I realized that this marked the first time in a long time that I had been truly alone.

No people, no screens, just *me*.

In that moment, some of the deepest questions of my soul began to surface:

What are you doing here?

What's wrong with you?

You are such a ____, you know that?

Can you just be better?

God, where are you?

I finally slowed down and became still enough to get to the root question: *God, where are you?*

I felt abandoned, alone, hopeless. I felt desperate for God to show up. Somehow, I had convinced myself that if God didn't shut the parties down himself, then he was absent. He didn't care.

But in that moment, I realized for the first time in a long time that I had just given God the *space* he needed to speak. I had not taken an inhale in our conversation for a long while.

The best part? When I gave him the space to speak, he spoke.

My Son, this is not the life that I want you to live. There is more. So much more! But you must spend time with me to discover it.

Wrecked.

I knew I'd heard the voice of the Lord. And I knew he was right. He had extended an invitation to solitude with no requirements other than to be with the Lord.

I wish I could say I accepted the invitation that night, but years would pass before I finally came to my end. For years, I fought back. The noise of this world constantly won my attention and drowned out the "still small voice" of the Lord.[15] Frankly, not until the last couple of years did I open and truly unpack the incredible gift of solitude.

Today, I've begun partaking in quarterly silent retreats, intentional getaways designed to detach from the noise and center my heart.

On these retreats, I've discovered a newfound love, joy, and peace in the Lord. I have experienced moments of deep anguish and delightful celebration. I've had moments of discovery and asked questions in the middle of the unknown. I've enjoyed moments of refreshment and endured moments of boredom. All these moments combined have created some beautiful experiences with the Lord.

But it takes *practice.*

Back to the Labyrinth

A world jam-packed with noise requires intentional practice if we are to develop a comfort with and desire for silence and solitude. Thankfully, we have thousands of years of church history to look back on that provide us tools that encourage us to seek times of silence and solitude.

Which brings me back to the labyrinth . . .

The labyrinth dates to the Middle Ages. Think of a maze with a planned pathway to the "end." Only, in this case, the end is the center. At the center, you find a series of items used to represent the presence of God. In my case, it's often three stumps (Father, Son, Spirit) and a bowl of smooth stones. I've used these stones over the years to write any words I've sensed the Lord has spoken to me.

Most monasteries, abbeys, or even the grounds of many Catholic churches have labyrinths. Visitors use the labyrinth to be still before God. Here's how to walk a prayer labyrinth:

1. Name your intention.

As you begin the labyrinth, name whatever you're seeking. Perhaps you seek answers to a question, clarity for a difficult situation, a material desire, or healing of some sort. Pray and ask God to be with you as you begin this journey. Ask him to show up.

In other words, *invite* Jesus into the space of solitude with you.

2. Walk the path.

As you walk, mull over your request, question, desire, or topic of conversation. Walk at a comfortable pace. There's no rush and you have nowhere to be. Don't force or rush a response from the Lord. Pay attention to your heart and soul.

What emotions get evoked?

What thoughts race through your mind?

Use a breath prayer (for example, "Lord, here I am") to center and re-center yourself as you journey to the middle. Use all these things as conversation points in your communion with God.

3. Give thanks.

As you enter the center, if you haven't gotten clarity on what you brought before the Lord, take some time to simply sit and be still. Believe that the Lord will speak. Ask and receive.

When you feel you've heard what the Lord has for you, mark the moment. Write down whatever you sensed him say. And then, say thank you. Use the time at the center to praise and worship God for who he is.

4. Reflect.

As you journey toward the beginning, reflect on whatever the Lord spoke over you. How will it change your mindset and heart posture as you reenter the world of noise? How will your centered heart interact differently with the scattered world around it?

Once you exit, finish by simply declaring, "So be it." In the church, we say, "Amen," which means, "Let it be."

Believe that God is who he says he is—and then trust him as you go forth.

Give It a Try

I understand that practicing solitude can feel uncomfortable at first. But give it a try!

Retreat for even five minutes in the morning. If you don't enjoy walking, then find a quiet place to sit and be still. And then, borrow the words of the prophet Samuel: "Speak, for your servant is listening."[16]

And then, *listen*.

Remove all distractions. Be still. And trust that in this space of grace, God will reveal himself to you.

If we are to get in step with the trail that God desires for us to blaze, we must first recover the practice of solitude and silence— especially in this world so driven by noise and distraction.

Consider this countercultural formation, my friend. We exist in a world full of noisy online echo chambers, incessant notifications, and constant background stimulation. When we retreat into silence, we dismiss the ethos of the world and enter unimpeded space with God. In the silence, many of us find the intimacy, clarity, and closeness from God that we, at our core, desperately long for.

When you feel lost, unsure, or stuck on the trail, solitude is the way back. Get alone with God, open your heart to him, and allow him to remind you of the Trailblazer he's called you to be.

6

DECELERATE AND LISTEN

Slowness

ON JULY 14, 2020, I found out just how sick I was.

Thankfully, I didn't have a physical illness, but it still caused me some real damage. I had a soul sickness, a hurry sickness.

The prior four months had gone by in a blur. Didn't they for everyone? On March 14, 2020, my world—and *the* world—literally shut down. The COVID-19 virus spread like wildfire and pushed everyone into isolation.

For many, this created an opportunity to stay home, enjoy family, and discover a new rhythm of life.

For me? I was a youth pastor in my first year of ministry and the axiom that best describes my response to a global shut down?

All gas, no brakes.

The world may have shut down, but how could the church shut down?

I went into panic mode ("I'm going to lose my job!") and then into performance mode ("I will make myself unexpendable"). In a way, it worked. I kept my job. In fact, *everyone* at our church kept their job, a huge credit to our amazing leadership.

But in another way, it failed entirely.

For four months, I isolated myself in a third-story apartment and worked ten- to twelve-hour days, six days a week (and sometimes, seven). If I couldn't find something to do, I'd make it up. If something needed to be done, I'd line up first to volunteer. I even spent four hours on a road trip making phone calls to 129 congregants while my poor wife had to listen.

No in-person gatherings? No problem.

We went from one gathering place for our students to six different virtual gathering opportunities throughout the week.

When the going got tough, I put my head down and just kept going.

Perhaps I should mention that I shared my office (I mean home) with my wife and puppy. For four months, my wife received the fumes of energy leftovers I had after working myself to the bone.

Nothing a two-week vacation in Colorado couldn't solve, right?

"Hurry is the great enemy of spiritual life in our day. You must ruthlessly eliminate hurry from your life."[1]

I'll never forget where I was when I first read those words from Dallas Willard. Sitting on the edge of a cliff, on a mountain in Colorado, by myself, I began weeping. It felt as if someone had taken a scalpel to my chest and cut out my heart.

I felt exhausted and saw no way out of my old pace of life. The easiest thing to do was run and retreat—which reminds me of an individual in Scripture who found himself in a similar position.

I'd like to introduce you to Elijah.

An Amazing Hot Streak

If you haven't read Elijah's story, you should.[2] Seriously, you're missing out.

This kick-butt prophet of Yahweh went on one of the greatest hot streaks of any individual in Scripture. Just look at this guy's résumé. In a two-chapter span of Scripture, he:

- Successfully predicted a great drought.[3]

- Received room service from wild ravens.[4]

- Supplied an endless amount of food for a widow and her son.[5]

- Raised the widow's son from the dead.[6]

- Took on 450 prophets of Baal (a pagan god).[7]

- Rained down fire from heaven.[8]

Elijah saw, experienced, and performed more miracles in this small stretch of ministry than many of us will see in our lifetime.

He was *busy.*

Busy doing the Lord's work.

Willard talks about ruthlessly eliminating hurry. Elijah took ruthlessness another way. He eliminated all 450 pagan prophets after showing them up on Mt. Carmel.[9]

That's what the young folks like to call "savage."

But then, things took a turn.

At the time, King Ahab and his wife, Jezebel, ruled Israel. Jezebel (or "Jezzy," as I like to call her) originally came from the pagan region of Tyre and Sidon. When she married Ahab, she reintroduced pagan worship into the Israelite community. Clearly, she didn't feel too happy to learn that Elijah had just slain 450 of her pagan prophets:

> Now Ahab told Jezebel everything Elijah had done and how he had killed all the prophets with the sword. So Jezebel sent a messenger to Elijah to say, "May the gods deal with me, be it ever so severely, if by this time tomorrow I do not make your life like that of one of them."[10]

Yikes.

Not a threat *I'd* ever like to receive. But surely, Elijah could handle it, right? I mean, here we have a prophet doing the Lord's work, witnessing and performing miracles left and right. Supernatural food delivery, raising the dead, and calling down fire from heaven, you name it. What could a pagan queen do in the face of a mighty prophet of God who could perform such amazing feats?

But Elijah's response doesn't particularly inspire:

> Elijah was afraid and ran for his life. When he came to Beersheba in Judah, he left his servant there, while he himself went a day's journey into the wilderness. He came to a broom bush, sat down under it and prayed that he might die. "I have had enough, LORD," he said. "Take my life; I am no better than my ancestors." Then he lay down under the bush and fell asleep.[11]

I read this and think, *what?* Do you feel as confused as I do? Surely, this isn't the same prophet we read about before. How could a man who saw, experienced, and participated in such mighty acts of divine deliverance get so fearful of some queen?

My opinion? He was in way over his head. Hurry had infected his soul.

I wonder if, in the middle of all those miracles, Elijah ever so slightly began to drift in his dependence and intimacy with the Lord? I wonder if the pace of his life, the many miracles and wondrous acts, created a relational chasm in his heart that equated the acts of God with the entire character of God?

Could it be that Elijah responded like someone in far too great a hurry?

Can you relate? I know I can.

Our world, especially in the West, seems consumed by hurry. We're hurry-sick. No one has taught me more about this problem than John Mark Comer.[12] So much of my formation around this idea of hurry (and following Jesus at large) has come from John Mark. He masterfully challenges us to embrace our limits and then lean into (as Peter Scazzero originally coined it) a "slow-down spirituality."[13]

We're on a journey to become Trailblazers. God has uniquely wired each of us in such a way that our influence and impact on this world can far outlast our lives. But are we willing to walk the difficult road to discover that purpose?

I say "walk" intentionally. Our culture obsesses over instant success. Hurry makes us believe that if we don't blow up on TikTok, Instagram Reels, or Twitter, well, we must not *really* be doing anything of substance.

The Japanese theologian Kosuke Koyama puts it this way in his book, *Three Mile an Hour God*:

> God walks "slowly" because he is love. If he is not love, he would have gone much faster. Love has its speed. It is an inner speed. It is a spiritual speed. It is a different kind of speed from the technological speed to which we are accustomed. It is "slow" yet it is lord over all other speeds since it is the speed of love.[14]

Genius.

May I ask the elephant-in-the-room question? When did five seconds of fame become more respectable than fifty years of faithfulness?

The impulse to hurry attracts us to the immediate, the glitzy, and the glamorous. But ruthlessly eliminating hurry isn't sexy. In fact, on the outside, it'll make your life look boring, simple . . . unimportant.

But what if you forsook the world to recover your soul? I think Jesus knew what he was talking about when he talked about our souls being more valuable than worldly profit.[15]

What if a slow pace is necessary to blaze the trail God called you to?

What if, in your ruthless elimination of hurry, you capture what has eluded you all along: a life of peace, intentionality, margin, community, and love?

That's the goal, isn't it?

Isn't that why we blaze this trail in the first place? To find our purpose and meaning in this life?

To become people of love?

But, as Comer states, "Hurry and love are incompatible."[16]

I think Elijah ran into this. Notice that after baring the last bit of his soul to the Lord, declaring an emptiness so great that he wants to die, he fell asleep.

How tired and exhausted must Elijah have felt? On the run for his life, in a position where his enemy might kill him at any moment, and yet he can't even keep his eyes open!

> All at once an angel touched him and said, "Get up and eat." He looked around, and there by his head was some bread baked over hot coals, and a jar of water. He ate and drank and then lay down again. The angel of the LORD came

back a second time and touched him and said, "Get up and eat, for the journey is too much for you." So he got up and ate and drank.[17]

In his kindness, the Lord offers to Elijah a type of soul rest that Elijah had … avoided? Eluded? Believing he was better than?

He took a soul rest of what I like to call "bed and bread."

Elijah's soul needed—more than anything hyperspiritual such as prayer, silence, Scripture, or fasting—bed and bread.

You have to love God, right? A God so tender and kind that, in our deepest moments of depletion, he offers a nap and nutrients.

Elijah wound up traveling to a mountain called Horeb, where he hid away in a cave. On that mountain the word of the Lord came to Elijah and said, "What are you doing here, Elijah?"[18]

Elijah immediately fired back: "I have been very zealous for the LORD God Almighty. The Israelites have rejected your covenant, torn down your altars, and put your prophets to death with the sword. I am the only one left, and now they are trying to kill me too."[19]

Then, it gets *really* good:

> The LORD said, "Go out and stand on the mountain in the presence of the LORD, for the LORD is about to pass by."
> Then a great and powerful wind tore the mountains apart and shattered the rocks before the LORD, but the LORD was not in the wind. After the wind there was an earthquake, but the LORD was not in the earthquake. After the earthquake came a fire, but the LORD was not in the fire. After the fire came a gentle whisper. When Elijah heard it, he pulled his cloak over his face and went out and stood at the mouth of the cave.
> Then a voice said to him, "What are you doing here, Elijah?"[20]

The story rivets me.

Elijah, on the run, attempted to live out of his performance-driven ministry that had carried him and his reputation so far. But then he ran out of gas. God found him in this cave and asked him, "What are you doing here?" Elijah immediately went into defense mode.

And then, God did a peculiar thing. He told Elijah that he would "pass by." Suddenly, a great and powerful wind whipped up. A *rush* of wind.

But God wasn't there.

Could God mean that his presence wanes when we get caught up in the rush of life?

Then an earthquake hit, and rocks began to split everywhere. How easy to get distracted by the mess created!

And yet, God wasn't in the earthquake.

Could God mean that his presence dissipates when distraction overcomes us?

Next came a fire. Did this event trigger Elijah? Did this fire remind him of the similar one he'd recently called down?

But the Lord wasn't in the fire.

Did this fire remind Elijah of the futility of living life through the lens of busyness and at the pace of hurry?

Eventually, Elijah heard a gentle whisper.

With Elijah's soul detoxed from rush, distraction, and busyness, I think God finally felt Elijah had reached a place to have a conversation. Why? Because God asked Elijah the very same question as before, and Elijah gave him the very same answer.[21]

The difference?

God responded.[22]

God gave Elijah instructions on how to finish blazing the trail the Lord had called him to travel. In his gentle whisper, the Lord commanded Elijah to anoint Elisha, the prophet who would succeed him. Elisha would carry on the tradition and message of Yahweh to the world after Elijah finished his run.

Perhaps Elijah's heart and soul had recovered to a pace and place where God could share with him next steps.

Do you find yourself on the run right now? Maybe life feels like a rat race. The hamster wheel never stops turning. You can't catch a breath.

What if God already has extended an invitation to the life you've always dreamed of living? But instead of requiring you to do more, hustle harder, and fill your calendar, you actually need to do *less?*

In this fast-paced age, to follow through with less amounts to a true act of courage. The urge to hurry will do whatever it can to convince you that more is . . . well, more. But the way of Jesus teaches us the "more" of "less." When we surrender our need to gain the whole world, we recover, hold on to, and strengthen something much more valuable . . . our soul.

The life you've always wanted to live, the trail you've been destined to blaze, lies right in front of you!

Those who go furthest and fastest in life accept their limits and blaze their unique trail. The way of the world, meanwhile, tries to convince us that the eight-lane highway is the fastest and most efficient route. But the world rarely warns us of the traffic jams and accidents ahead.

Take a deep breath. Slow down.

And blaze the trail God's called *you* to.

How Did I Get Here?

My mountaintop experience came at a particularly low point in my life, never more evident than when I entered the bedroom later that night. My wife and I were on a much-needed vacation during a busy season.

I sat down on the bed next to my wife, wearing a face that non-verbally communicated, "Ask me what I did today."

For whatever reason, she didn't read it. So, finally, I spoke up.

"You'll never guess what happened to me today." As I spoke, I began to slide my hand onto her leg . . . (don't worry, this stays PG).

Immediately, she withdrew and with a face of absolute disgust, looked at me and said, "What are you doing?"

"I'm trying to talk to you."

"No, I mean, what are you doing? With your hand? Micah, you haven't pursued me like that in months."

Gut punch.

Here I sat, attempting to tell my wife about all the wonderful wisdom I'd gleaned from Comer, Scazzero, and Willard on my mountain-hike day and instead got the message that the compulsion to hurry owned my life.

That was a wake-up call.

And this was day six of our ten-day trip. It had taken me six days to even get to a place where I could slow down my mind enough to attempt (miserably) to engage with my wife.

How did I get here?

I spent the rest of our trip attempting to figure that out. And upon our return, I resolved to blaze a trail of slowness in our home. With the world hurrying around me, I needed systems and practices in place to help me slow down.

Four Rhythms to Oust Busyness

At one time, futurists and sociologists predicted that by the twenty-first century, personal productivity would allow for work weeks of twenty-five to thirty hours. This, they insisted, would become a cultural norm.

We've gone the opposite way instead.

We work more, harder, and longer than ever before.[23] We've seen rates of suicide, depression, anxiety, and other mental health illnesses rise to highs not seen since 1932, at the height of the Great Depression.

It makes you wonder: Has our pace of life pushed us beyond our limits? Has our sphere and span of access overloaded our minds, hearts, and souls?

Every time a public figure takes his or her life (or attempts to), this conversation comes up.

Any instance of extreme cyberbullying or mass shooting brings these conversations to the forefront.

Every time a friend credits a divorce to "growing apart," we feel it.

Each headline about a fellow pastor burning out, self-selecting out, or sinning out of ministry elicits this ache.

Every time we witness an absent parent, we see it.

We recognize the dangers that our pace of life presents, and yet very few of us seem willing to do anything about it.

And so, as followers of Jesus, we find ourselves in the middle of a society addicted to speed, efficiency, and production, living in a culture consumed by image, reputation, and status.

And it's literally killing us.

Worse, we don't know what to do about it. So, we feel overwhelmed and resign ourselves to the way things are. That's just the way it's going to be. Right?

But what if it didn't have to be that way? What if we could expel the urge to hurry and instead slow down? Is it even possible?

Consider four rhythms that I believe can help oust busyness, distraction, and hurry, and instead help to center your soul so you can hear the still, small voice of God.

1. Master your phone.
Have you ever found yourself halfway to an event, realized you forgot your phone, and turned around to retrieve it—even at the expense of being late?

Just me? Sweet.

But we've all been there, haven't we?

It amazes me how culturally acceptable it has become to remain constantly tethered to our devices. We no longer even hold people accountable for being rude. We order food, grocery shop, and walk around public spaces with our faces glued to screens.

I spoke with a pastor a while back who told me that a friend of his in HR got interrupted by a young lady he was *interviewing for a job* when she answered her ringing phone and asked to step out of the interview to catch up with a friend.

And we've *normalized* this.

I'm convinced there's a better way to live.

Listen, I'm thankful for technology. I use technology often. I'm writing this on a (albeit old and beat-up) MacBook Air. So, I don't want this to sound hyperidealistic. I'm not suggesting that we should all go off-grid. I do think, however, we ought to take an honest assessment.

Who runs your life? You? Or your phone?

The smartphone has made it virtually impossible to establish healthy boundaries. We've essentially become available and accessible 24/7, 365. Cal Newport said it best: "Humans are not wired to be constantly wired."[24]

We worship a Savior (fully God and fully human, remember?) who often retreated to lonely places. *Something* doesn't add up.

One way to slow down? Master your phone.

Take off email, games, and other mindless distractions.

Turn off your notifications and create set times for checking in. I think it will amaze you, as it did me, to see how little you're actually needed.

If you want to get *really* frisky, change your phone settings to a black and white display. My first two years of college, I set my home screen to lifehacker.com (don't judge). I wanted to be the best version of myself as I entered adulthood, and I figured life hacking was my way to do it.

I remember reading an article citing Tristan Harris—notable ex-design ethicist at Google and mindful technology guru—discussing how grayscale mode on your smartphone could curb your technology addiction.[25] I tried it on and off for a few years, but in the last few years have really settled into it.

Whatever it takes to ensure that you remain in charge of your phone and not the other way around, I'd encourage you to try it.

Technology in itself, like money, is amoral, neither good nor bad. But if you allow it to infiltrate your life in excess, expect serious consequences to your mental health.[26]

Put the phone down and . . .

2. Begin the day in quiet.
This has been a game changer for me. Let me give you two scenarios to illustrate what I mean:

SCENARIO #1:
Alarm goes off. You roll over and pick up your phone. The dreaded email comes: you forgot the big project. Your boss is not happy.

Your day is effectively ruined.

SCENARIO #2:
Alarm goes off. You slowly get out of bed. You find a quiet corner in your place and open the Scriptures. Peace, love, and joy cascade into your soul.

You get ready and settle into work mode. The dreaded email comes: you forgot the big project. Your boss is not happy.

Your day, while difficult, can be navigated with a centered heart.

Same circumstances, different outcome.

The difference? Your start.

Every waking moment battles for your attention. Your thoughts, your words, and your actions—along with everyone else's—fight for your attention.

But what if God won *every single day*? What if he received your first moments of attention? As we've seen from Elijah, God loves to speak to the quiet, settled soul.

Could a practice like this slow down the rest of your day?

3. Rediscover the gift of a walk.
Perhaps more than any other practice over the last couple of years, the subtle rhythm of a walk has transformed my daily life. Almost every day, rain or shine or snow, I try to take at least a one-mile walk around my neighborhood. No screens, no distractions, and nowhere to be.

Rylei will often join me for an uninterrupted, fully present conversation.

On these walks I find my mind slowing down as I review the day, contemplate, and remain prayerfully aware of God's voice. I stop and look at leaves, pay attention to the wildlife scurrying around, or look to the sky and daydream through the clouds.

Walks, for me, have become daily Mount Horeb encounters. I set aside the distractions, hurry, and busyness that my soul has built up and eventually find myself centered to converse with God.

4. Enjoy the blessing that is Sabbath.

If you engage in these daily disciplines, slow down, and crave more, then you may yearn to recover the internal rhythm that God instituted: six days of work and one day of rest. To recover the Sabbath.

Shabbat.

At this point, two questions may float to the top of your mind. First, what *is* Sabbath?

In the beginning, God made the heavens and the earth. For six days, God created the fish of the sea, the birds of the air, the trees, and the stars. He also created human beings. But on the seventh day, he rested. Genesis 2 says,

> Thus the heavens and the earth were completed in all their vast array. By the seventh day God had finished the work he had been doing; so on the seventh day he rested from all his work. Then God blessed the seventh day and made it holy, because on it he rested from all the work of creating that he had done.[27]

God took a step back from his work and enjoyed it. On the seventh day, God left space and room to rest, a twenty-four-hour period of unhurried delight with no have-tos or ought-tos, resulting in deep rest and renewal.

Sabbath is a gift from God, meant for us to receive. Jesus tells us, "The Sabbath was made for man, not man for the Sabbath."[28]

Sabbath is a gift to enjoy!

Shabbat literally means "to cease." To stop. To slow down. To be present.

Second question: How do I *practice* Sabbath? How do I do it?

Let me suggest (and forgive me for stating the obvious) that you look to Jesus. Study the rhythms in which he lived his life.

Jesus did not wait until everyone got properly cared for. He didn't wait until all who sought him got healed. He did not ask permission to go, nor did he leave anyone behind, "on call," or even let his disciples know where he intended to go.

Jesus obeyed a deeper rhythm.

When the moment for rest had come, the time for healing had ended. He would simply stop, retire to a quiet place, and pray.

Study the life of Jesus and how he obeyed the deeper rhythm of our souls. How he routinely surrendered and submitted his life to God.

Another key? Start small.

If a twenty-four-hour period of rest seems like a daunting task, that's okay! Begin with an hour, a morning, or an afternoon of intentional *rest.* Listen to your body and your soul and obey that deeper rhythm. When you sense the time has come to rest, retreat and rest with the intention of coming back and ENGAGING your congregation, your spouse, your children, or your friends as a person of grace, peace, and love.

Finally, develop consistency.

Because we are rhythmic creatures, we respond well to consistency. Even if it's just an hour every Friday, protect that hour. Make that a sacred hour to retreat and rest and pray!

Know that there's no "right" way to practice Sabbath. What's restful for me may certainly not be restful for you . . . and that's okay.

Trying to do a full dive into Sabbath in this small amount of time is virtually impossible; but I hope, at the very least, I've introduced you (or reintroduced you) to a God who cares about your longevity.

My friend, the work you're doing matters and God wants you to last. He wants you to enjoy and find fulfillment in your calling. He wants you to be the mother or father, husband or wife, pastor or parishioner, the *Trailblazer* that you've been called to be!

And to become that person means surrendering our selfish motives and desires for incessant hurry. It means routinely retreating to the quiet place, to remember that there is a God . . . and that you are not him, as John Ortberg says.

A Marvel Like Nothing Else

For many months prior to the conversation Ry and I had in Colorado, I was too hurried to really engage and pursue her.

I wonder: Are we often so hurried that we miss God? Oh, what a tragedy!

My friend, we serve an invitational God, a God who *wants* and *desires* to commune with us.

Root out the impulse to hurry! You won't find God in the rush of the wind, the distraction of the earthquake, or the busyness of the fire. He invites you to come to him, to get away with him, to walk— s l o w l y —and to watch how he lives life.

A life of unforced rhythms of grace.

When we keep company with him, we learn to hear his voice. And when we keep his company, we find true life, both freely and lightly.

Then we can recover our soul in the slow, still company of Christ. In stillness and slowness, we can quietly cut through layers of noise, notifications, and information, and rediscover the unique invitation extended to us.

God has given you a unique purpose. Resist the temptation to take your cues from the culture around you.

Fight tooth and nail to remain connected to the Vine, Jesus, and allow his life to transform your own into a marvel like nothing else.

7

ALWAYS CHOOSE TO BE BRAVE
Courage

I have always felt that ultimately along the way of life an individual must stand up and be counted and be willing to face the consequences, whatever they are. And if he is filled with fear he cannot do it. My great prayer is always for God to save me from the paralysis of crippling fear, because I think when a person lives with the fears of the consequences for his personal life he can never do anything in terms of lifting the whole of humanity and solving many of the social problems which we confront in every age and every generation.[1]

These are the words of Dr. Martin Luther King Jr. They stopped me in my tracks when I first read them in his autobiography.

For hundreds of pages, King tells story after story about the tremendous courage he, and the entire Black community, showed in protesting racial injustice. Whether it was Rosa Parks refusing to move from her bus seat, King's residence getting bombed, or the hundreds of peaceful protesters beaten, doused by firetruck hoses, and attacked by police dogs, these men and women showed courageous resolve and restraint.

After the bombing (which took place while King's wife, Coretta, and oldest daughter were at home), King reflects on his interaction with several white reporters, city commissioners, and the mayor. They felt "sorry this unfortunate incident had taken place in our city."[2]

King, taking internal inventory of his heart, said to himself, "You must not allow yourself to become bitter."[3]

Magnificent courage in the face of destructive adversity.

King displayed remarkable courage under the constant threat of assassination—which happened, too, on April 4, 1968. His courage allowed him to blaze a trail toward equality, dignity, and unity for an entire people group. Our country and world at large still feel the ripple effects of Dr. King's courageous actions.

We've seen similar legacies before, and we can learn much from them again, if we're willing to step into it. So, where do we begin?

How about with a certain Jewish queen who found herself at the center of an extermination plot?

Now, *That's* a Problem

Esther's story begins in a strange way. As a Jewish orphan, adopted by her cousin, living in Persia, she appears in antiquity's version of *The Bachelor*. She makes up part of a group of women who compete to marry the king of Persia and so become queen. Esther finds favor with the eunuch in charge of these "contestants" and eventually wins the heart of the king himself.

In true rags-to-riches fashion, Esther finds herself in the most influential relationship in the entire kingdom.[4] Think Meghan Markle and Prince Harry on steroids. Esther is THE Queen.

But she has a problem.

Esther's husband is a ruthless tyrant. This man kicked his ex-wife out of the palace for disobedience to his self-indulgent wishes.[5] And Esther, a Jew, secretly belongs to a despised social class, which most likely (had he known) would have excluded her from company with the king in the first place. Her husband, the king, has no clue about her true ethnicity.[6] Her reluctance to be fully transparent laid the foundation for a deadly future challenge.

After a personal rift between Mordecai (Esther's cousin) and Haman (the king's second-in-command), the Jews find themselves threatened with extinction. In a rage, Haman convinces the king to exterminate the entire Jewish population because of Mordecai's refusal to bow before him.[7]

Esther now becomes fully entangled in a political nightmare. Her husband has agreed to an evil plan to destroy her people.

What should she do?

To Mordecai, it's simple: tell your husband, the king, the truth. Inform him of your Jewish heritage and beg him to terminate the edict that commands the genocide of the Jewish people.

Be *courageous*. Save us!

Esther didn't feel so sure.

She tells Mordecai that anyone who appears before the king without receiving a summons, even her, invites possible execution. Remember, this tyrant king already has banished his ex-wife for a trifle. He has history.

And then, Mordecai delivers the most critical line in the book of Esther. He tells her,

> Do not think that because you are in the king's house you alone of all the Jews will escape. For if you remain silent at this time, relief and deliverance for the Jews will arise from

another place, but you and your father's family will perish. And who knows but that you have come to your royal position *for such a time as this?*[8]

What a line.

In other words, "Esther, you must decide whether you're willing to overcome your fear or if you'll allow the 'what-ifs?' to consume you."

Oh, how we can relate! You have this burning conviction to go after that promotion.

But what if I don't get picked?

You long to ask him or her out for coffee.

But what if they say no?

An internal compulsion drives you to go back to school and get that degree.

But what if I fail?

Fear drives so many of us from ever stepping onto the trail that God calls us to blaze. Somehow, we persuade ourselves that our conviction and God's calling simply don't match. Whatever the deep ache within us might be, we feel certain that we'll never *really* have what it takes to do anything about it.

And so, we wait.

And wait.

And . . . wait.

And then we miss it.

Our fear causes us to forfeit God's invitation to become a Trailblazer.

Esther's time to blaze a trail has come. Will she cower in fear or courageously choose to step into her calling? She's reached the dreaded fork-in-the-road moment. Will she go left or go right?

What would *we* do?

What if we got it wrong?

Fair questions, to be sure. But what if the only wrong choice is to not choose at all?

I'll never forget the day a friend introduced this concept to me. At that moment I decided to blaze the trail that led me to writing these words.

What Am I Supposed to Do?

A terrifying time hit me in February of 2019. Eight months earlier, I convinced my wife of three whole weeks to move from the community where we'd spent the last four years,[9] to a town of 15,000 strangers in the middle of Nowhere, Illinois.[10]

Hear my pitch: "Babe, I have the opportunity to go play basketball at a different school. And on *this* team, I'll get to shoot a lot more shots, score a lot more points, which will mean a lot more happiness for your new husband. What do ya say?"

Graciously, she agreed (although the selfish motives behind it did not make her a huge fan). The next eight months were a blur of fun, discovery, hardship, and breakthrough.

If you like reality TV, you wouldn't need *The Bachelor* or the book of Esther. Just roll the tape of two newly married twenty-one-year-olds in a 600-square-foot house, all by themselves. Sparks flew (and I don't mean exclusively in the romantic sense).

Those eight months greatly challenged us but also profoundly formed us.

About eight months into the adventure, we had just started to find our groove. Basketball season had almost ended, Rylei had settled into her job, we were finding friends, planning out our first summer of marriage, etc. All seemed right in the world.

And then the phone rang.

Out of nowhere, I received an invitation to apply to become the next high school pastor at a megachurch in Indianapolis, Indiana. In an instant, my world got turned upside down.

The life we had imagined, the life we'd dreamed of, the life we had planned, didn't—in any way, shape, or form—involve a move back to Indianapolis so soon. But we agreed to pray about it.

A few days later, Rylei and I showed up at our pastor's house for a prescheduled dinner. They had barely set the salad down on the table before I unleashed a monologue about our predicament.

"Pastor Brian, you don't understand . . . our life is *awesome* here. We love it. I get to play basketball, go to school, and hang out with friends. Rylei has a pretty undemanding job with a lot of flexibility and free time to pursue her own passions. Life is *great*.

"But now, we have this other opportunity, and to go that route would mean uprooting our family *again*, giving up my last year of college basketball—the year I've worked my whole career for—giving up the pursuit of my college degree in the classroom setting, and leaving the friends and family we've gained and grown to love in this town.

"WHAT AM I SUPPOSED TO DO?"

I sat there, at my pastor's table, with what felt like the biggest crossroads of my entire life in front of me. Whatever decision *we* made wouldn't affect only me anymore. I now had a wife, a family, to take care of.

"Pastor Brian, what if I make the wrong decision? What if I'm prayerful and discerning and I choose to stay and I should've gone? What if I go and I should've stayed?"

Brian pulled out a napkin and a pen. (Isn't that how *Harry Potter* started? I hoped whatever he was about to write would be as good.)

On this napkin he drew two intersecting lines.

"Micah, right now you're here, at a crossroads. You could go left or you could go right. But either way, so long as you're prayerful and discerning, so long as your motives are pure, so long as you pursue obedience to Jesus first, *whatever* decision you make will be the *right* one."

And with some of the greatest pastoral kindness and gentleness ever spoken to me, Brian said something that changed the trajectory of my life. His words freed me to courageously step into the unknown.

"Micah, God is a *bender*, not a *breaker*. He's powerful enough to bend you back to the straight and narrow Way of Jesus, should you choose to disobey him here. He's also powerful enough to use your good intentions, your pure motives, and your honest ambitions to change the world, even if it's not the route you were 'supposed' to choose. The destination isn't the decision; the destination is getting to a place of unequivocal, sold-out, faith, trust, and obedience in Jesus that forms and shapes you into an authentic follower of him."

Absolute gold. I was undone.

I had to make a choice. I had to trust that God would do something great with or without my participation in either basketball or ministry.

But where, in my heart of hearts, did I feel the Lord leading us?

It Comes Down to Your Theology of God

Do you see the same kind of language from Pastor Brian that Mordecai used with Esther? Let me remind you:

> Do not think that because you are in the king's house you alone of all the Jews will escape. For *if you remain silent at this time, relief and deliverance for the Jews will arise from*

another place, but you and your father's family will perish. And who knows but that you have come to your royal position for such a time as this?[11]

It really comes down to your theology of God.

Do you believe that he is who he says he is? That he's in control? That he's good? That he has your best in mind?

If you answer yes, then when he asks you to courageously blaze a trail, you must overcome your fear and push forward.

If you answer no, then you'll never experience the full depth and breadth of God's goodness, power, and mercy.

And you know what? Either way, it won't stop God from being God.

Pay attention to the emphasized words of Mordecai: *"If you remain silent at this time, relief and deliverance for the Jews will arise from another place, but you and your father's family will perish."*[12]

In other words, "Esther, if you don't do this, someone else will."

"Micah, if you don't surrender your basketball career and accept this position, someone else will."

If you don't go for that promotion, someone else will.

If you don't ask him or her out, someone else will.

If you don't go after that degree, someone else will.

You choose.

Courage or fear? Inhale . . . Exhale . . .

I know this may feel a tad touchy. Please, hear my heart. Too often, we mistake our inaction for God's absence. Just because God doesn't deliver, provide, or carry out his will on your timeline or in the way that you think he should, doesn't mean he's not present.

What if he's simply looking for someone to partner with?

What if he's holding onto the hope that his glory can shine through a broken, backwards person?

What if he wants *you* to blaze the trail?

My friend, you have what it takes. You've been born for such a time as this.

What ache stirs within your soul? Go after your dream! Start somewhere, today. Because if you don't, life is but a vapor and before you know it, the trail God's called you to blaze will be too far in the past for you to take it and through it form a legacy.

In those fork-in-the-road moments, where either option feels terrifying—*choose.*

Choose courage.

Choose to believe that the God who has seen you to this moment will also see you through it.

This was Esther's moment to step onto the trail that God had called her to blaze. We still talk about her today because of how she responded. Mordecai had dropped his legendary line; now, it was Esther's turn:

> Go, gather together all the Jews who are in Susa, and fast for me. Do not eat or drink for three days, night or day. I and my attendants will fast as you do. When this is done, I will go to the king, even though it is against the law. And if I perish, I perish.[13]

Goose bumps.

This feels like an exchange straight out of a movie, doesn't it? Esther puts her courage on full display. She can step into this moment, or she can allow it to pass her by. She'll probably die either way. Nonetheless, she chooses the courageous route, the trail to blaze, for such a time as this.

Can you sense the conviction formed in Esther's heart? She's choosing to trust the God who sees.[14] She's ready to step onto the trail and blaze a new path, even if it means giving up her life.

Three days and a few wine-and-dine events later, the fateful moment arrives:

> So the king and Haman went to Queen Esther's banquet, and as they were drinking wine on the second day, the king again asked, "Queen Esther, what is your petition? It will be given you. What is your request? Even up to half the kingdom, it will be granted."
>   Then Queen Esther answered, "If I have found favor with you, Your Majesty, and if it pleases you, grant me my life— this is my petition. And spare my people—this is my request. For I and my people have been sold to be destroyed, killed and annihilated."[15]

Esther's words rock the king's world. In a fury, he brings justice on Haman, honors both Esther and Mordecai, and provides a creative way out for the Jews from the oppressive edict.[16] The Jews are allowed to protect themselves from harm. The new edict saves God's people from annihilation.[17]

All of this came to pass because of a courageous choice made by Esther. She believed Mordecai's words that God had placed her in this position "for such a time as this."

Esther's courage preceded her people's jubilant deliverance:

> The city of Susa held a joyous celebration. For the Jews it was a time of happiness and joy, gladness and honor. In every province and in every city to which the edict of the king came, there was joy and gladness among the Jews, with feasting and celebrating.[18]

What is God calling you to do for such a time as this? Are you willing to courageously step into the unknown and find out?

A Blueprint for a Courageous Life

Esther's life offers us a blueprint for how to wade uncharted waters courageously. Once she accepts Mordecai's challenge, she turns first to *fasting*. She asks Mordecai and other Jews to fast for three days alongside of her. Esther begins with fasting to help her develop the courage necessary to move forward.

Through fasting, we surrender our will to God's will. Fasting creates an environmental crucible for supernatural courage to develop.

I love how New Testament scholar and theologian Scot McKnight frames it. He says, "fasting is what happens in the Bible when Israelites and Christians surrender the entire person—heart, soul, mind, spirit, and body—to God."[19] In this posture of total surrender, we receive the strength to press onward toward whatever God calls us to.

It's no coincidence that Jesus fasted for forty days and forty nights before entering public ministry.[20] That period became a formative crucible for courage, the kind of courage he leaned on when facing a brutal execution.[21]

If you find yourself fighting some fear regarding your future, may I encourage you to lean into fasting? For twenty-four hours (or more), surrender all food and drink as you consecrate your heart, soul, mind, spirit, and body to the Lord. Believe, in faith, that God will form in you the courage required as you step into full dependence on him.

The Bible doesn't tell us what transpired within that three-day fast for Esther. All we know is that after the three days, she began a process that led to her asking the big question—a question that could have led to her death.

Where else could she have forged her courage except in the fire of the fast?

One Step at a Time

Blazing a trail is hard work. Reasons exist why no one has traveled it before. To clear the path, you'll have to remove everything standing in your way.

Not sure what that looks like? Think of blazing a literal path through a forest. How would you do it?

Imagine you're Lewis and Clark. A vast, dense forest lies before you. You carry a canteen, a (blank) map, and a machete.

How will you make it through? It's not a trick question . . .

The answer? *One step at a time.*

Suppose God has laid a desire on your heart to teach under-privileged kids in Africa. Should you book the plane ticket today and go?

Probably not.

But can you begin researching what it would take to move closer to making that goal a reality?

Absolutely.

Or perhaps you have a God-given desire to open a coffee shop or start a fashion brand. Should you quit your job and step fully into trying to make that happen, with no experience and limited resources?

Again, probably not.

Think back to Esther. She *knew* what she needed to do, but she took it one step at a time. Only after she prepared herself for what came next did she step obediently onto the trail God had asked her to blaze.

I hope and pray that you don't read this book as some idealistic dreamscape. We're interacting with *real* people, with *real* stories, who made *real*, *courageous* decisions despite lives full of mistakes, brokenness, sin, and strife.

We're after beauty in the brokenness, miracles in the mundane.

Remember the dream you wrote down in chapter 2? Write it out again, this time with any modifications you see that you may need to make:

MY DREAM:

_____

_____

_____

_____

_____

_____

_____

_____

_____

Now, what one step can you take to courageously move toward that dream?

It may mean fasting, praying, and asking the Lord to confirm the dream within you.

It may be more tangible: quitting the job, selling the house, taking out the loan.

Whatever it may be, we're after the *next* courageous decision that God is calling you to make.

The life you've always wanted is within reach, but you must be willing to step into it. Remember, God is invitational by nature. He won't force his way in. He asks you to courageously accept whoever he's called you to be, to pursue the unique purpose he's given you.

And then?

Live it, one step at a time.

As you move, God will assure.

Have courage and take heart, says Jesus.[22] If God has seen you to it, he will see you through it.[23]

8

TAKE CHARGE OF YOUR DAY

Discipline

"WHAT'D YOU EAT FOR BREAKFAST?" my coach asked.

"A bagel," a player replied.

"No, son. I said, 'What'd you eat for breakfast?'"

"I ate a bagel."

My teammates could barely hold it together. They knew what was coming.

"Son, what'd you eat for breakfast?"

"I ate a bagel, coach."

This conversation took place every year in college between my head coach and one of our freshman basketball players during our first week of summer practices. Imagine being a nervous, eighteen-year-old kid, already overwhelmed with trying to find your classes and adjust to life away from home, and knowing that you're about to be brutally introduced to the physicality of college basketball—and then your coach starts yelling at you about what you ate for breakfast before a 5:30 a.m. practice.

"Boys, he ate a bagel. What should he have eaten?"

The upperclassmen would shout, "The Word!" and everyone (but the freshman) would laugh.

Coach T[1] would then say, "The Word. We always eat the Word for breakfast. A filled-up soul is worth more to you than a filled-up stomach before a day's work begins."

Every day, 4:45 a.m. came *real* early. We had to wake up by then to be on the court by 5:25 ("on time" or "wildcat time," as it was non-affectionately called) for our 5:30 a.m. practice. After practice came six to eight hours of classes, followed by another practice, then homework, then bed. And then you'd do it all over again.

This was my life during the months of June and October all throughout college. #2-a-dayszn (that's Gen-Z speak for "two-a-day-season").

So, why a 4:45 a.m. wake-up call?

You had to wake up by then to implement the fifteen-minute buffer for quiet time with the Lord before your day's work began.

"A filled-up soul is worth more to you than a filled-up stomach."

I played for a college basketball program that amassed a 93–20 record with two national championships from 2015–2018. But all of that was secondary to what we were eating for breakfast before practice.

Our coaches never focused on the last play, the last practice, or the last game. They never focused on the next play, the next practice, or the next game. Always, to begin practice, they focused on prayer and the Word of God. In that environment my coaches forged and shaped me.

Discipline paved the way for success.

But really, that's nothing new, is it?

Success Doesn't Happen by Itself

If you look to the great icons of our world—Steve Jobs, Michael Jordan, C. S. Lewis, Serena Williams, Chance the Rapper, and more—what will you find?

A meticulously disciplined person. We know instinctively that success doesn't happen without hard work.

We reward those who execute their craft at a high level. "Board man gets paid,"[2] once quipped the soft-spoken Kawhi Leonard. And you know what? The world loved it. Because we *agree*!

And yet, how many of us believe the same thing about the spiritual life?

Crickets.

For some reason, a theology has trickled into the Western church that says, "Go to church on Sundays, live life how you want to Monday through Saturday, repeat, and you will *grow*." Where's the discipline in that? In what other area of our lives do we believe a devoted hour per week will make us better?

A 2018 study[3] found that we spend an average of an hour and forty-two minutes *per week* on the toilet.

I'll just leave that there.

We've become so accustomed to hearing and learning about the grace of Jesus that we've equated his death on the cross to win our eternal salvation with a no-effort-required theology that can make us more whole, holy, and healthy.[4] That's dangerous, my friend.

Jesus prayed that we would experience God's Kingdom and will on earth as it is in heaven. But we regularly experience the Kingdom of God only by routinely *choosing* to experience the Kingdom of God. Yes, the Kingdom of God is being formed and fashioned all around us. You're bound to run into it on occasion (think miracles, healings, provision, presence, etc.), but to truly experience life to the full requires a daily choice to forsake the way of this world and to submit to the way of Jesus. And that takes effort.

I love how Paul puts it in Romans 12:

> Do not be conformed to this world, but be transformed
> by the renewal of your mind, that by testing you may discern
> what is the will of God, what is good and acceptable
> and perfect.[5]

That is our charge. If we are to discern the trail that God calls us to blaze, we must get in the right headspace to step onto it, endure when trials come, and overcome through the power of the Holy Spirit. To do this requires time, experience, practice, and history.

It makes me think of the college students who get to shoot half-court shots on ESPN's *College Gameday*. Have you ever seen it? If not, it's well worth thirty seconds of your time. Tune in on Saturday mornings at 11:50 a.m. EST during the fall and winter months.

Do these "regular" college students hit the vastly difficult half-court shot? Not often, but sometimes they do.

Now, imagine if we sent Stephen Wardell Curry II (that's NBA superstar Steph Curry, if you don't know) to half court. How long do you think it would take him to hit one?

Answer: not long.

Why do we have so much more confidence in Steph Curry to

make that shot than in a "regular" college student? Because he's disciplined himself to make that shot routinely.

In the same way, we must overcome our impulse toward laziness that says, "It'll just come. The peace, the love, the joy, the fulfillment you want to feel, it'll come one day." It sounds crazy when we say it out loud, but how many of us believe that?

My friend, to become a Trailblazer, you must become a person of discipline. Someone who routinely chooses to commune with God. Remember, out of our *being* with God comes greater *doing* for God. We can't mix this up.

Will we get lucky from time to time if we do mix it up? Sure. But throughout Scripture, we see men and women who blaze trails out of an overflow of zeal and passion for God. That's not manufactured hype. It's water from a deep well. Pastor Jon Tyson—or "JT Money" as he likes to be called[6]—likens spiritual zeal to a "reservoir that overflows." What a beautiful word picture!

One person stands out in Scripture regarding his disciplined life. Over and over in his story we see a direct correlation between his discipline and God's deliverance.

Disciplined Daniel blazes a trail like none other. And his story invites us to do the same.

Allegiance to God or to This World?

Our first introduction to Daniel presents him in an uncomfortable position *very* familiar to many of us today: having to decide whether to give our allegiance to God or to this world.

Surely, *we'd* choose allegiance to God, right? But if your day-to-day life looks anything like mine, you know that doesn't always happen.

Daniel shows us a better way.

He mesmerizes me with his ability to both serve under a pagan dictator *and* honor and uphold the way of the Lord. And he's deliberate about it.

Babylon, an ancient superpower, had taken Daniel captive along with many other Israelite exiles. Because Daniel came from a family of privilege,[7] the Babylonians selected him to live among their elites and to be indoctrinated into their pagan culture, which included an assigned nutrition plan. Think of a college football player who needs to maintain a certain physique. Daniel's position provided him with a Babylonian plan for healthy development.

The problem? This meal plan didn't honor God.

Jewish food customs insisted that to partake in the king's assigned food and drink plan would "defile"[8] or corrupt Daniel's soul. Daniel would have found it *so* easy to simply eat and drink whatever the king provided—but Daniel refused to settle. And here we see the power of discipline and the fuel it supplies to help us effectively blaze a trail.

For ten days, Daniel and his three friends arrange to eat a diet of vegetables and water only. "Then compare our appearance with that of the young men who eat the royal food," Daniel tells his supervisor, "and treat your servants in accordance with what you see."[9]

After ten days, the four men "looked healthier and better nourished than any of the young men who ate the royal food."[10]

What is this? A subtle ad for veganism?

No.

It's a testament to the power of discipline as a potent character trait.

The impulse toward laziness pulls at us to settle and compromise to gain ease and comfort. But discipline has an unrelenting commitment to uphold a particular standard. For Daniel and his friends, that standard meant abstaining from royal food and drink.

We see this pattern throughout Daniel's life. Discipline becomes a crucial aspect of his character formation.

Decades later, Daniel continues to hold a high position in the court of the king. Only by now, he serves under new leadership.

Darius has replaced Nebuchadnezzar as ruler of Babylon. In an effort to establish his reign, he implements a new leadership hierarchy. And who sits at the very top?

Daniel.

Daniel had distinguished himself so much among the nation's administrators (called "satraps") because of his abilities that the king was going to promote him over the whole kingdom.[11] But that plan immediately encountered resistance from the other administrators. Their jealousy and insecurity led them to propose a subversive decree, designed to flatter the king and dispose of Daniel: "Anyone who prays to any god or human being during the next thirty days, except to you, Your Majesty, shall be thrown into the lions' den."[12]

Darius saw the law as yet another way to establish his power in the kingdom he now ruled.

Consider that bad boy signed and dated.

But this news put in grave jeopardy Daniel's life and habits. It should terrify a disciplined man of prayer to lose the legal ability to pray, right?

Not Daniel.

Laziness could so easily have tempted him:

Hey, it's just thirty days.

You can pick it up again after the edict runs its course.

You could use a break, anyway.

But Daniel had deeply ingrained the trait of discipline into his life. His response shows as much:

> Now when Daniel learned that the decree had been
> published, he went home to his upstairs room where the

windows opened toward Jerusalem. Three times a day he got down on his knees and prayed, giving thanks to his God, just as he had done before.[13]

Goodness.

We might as well call him, "Don't-Blink Daniel." The edict didn't even faze him. Why not?

Because his discipline drove him.

Three times a day, every day, Daniel went home, kneeled in an upstairs room, and prayed at the window that looked toward Jerusalem. Without fail. Now, practicing a discipline with no consequence on the line is tough enough. But to throw in a life-endangering threat?

I'm out.

I mean—I don't want to be—but it'd certainly cross my mind.

Wouldn't it cross yours too?

I've thought about this as I've watched my brothers and sisters in Christ in Afghanistan, China, Syria, and other places get persecuted or even executed for their profession of faith in Christ. And I've wondered, *Would I be willing to do that? Do I have the discipline to withstand that level of persecution? Is my commitment to Jesus really that strong?*

In my most honest, vulnerable response . . . I'd hope so. But in reality, our Western way of life has left many of us seriously mal-formed with respect to suffering. Many of us don't really know what it's like to have something of value on the line.

But others of us do.

Has your value system ever cost you a job or a promotion?

Has your spouse left you because of your faith?

Have godly decisions led to you being estranged from your family?

Have you suffered a terrible accident or gotten very sick while serving on a mission trip?

I don't know your story. In general, however, most of us have never had to face death for the sake of the cross. That's why we should so appreciate Daniel's discipline in this moment.

The biblical text doesn't give us even a hint of pause on Daniel's part. Apparently, he thinks, *I'm a follower of God and I pray to him three times a day.*

Get it. Got it. Done.

But Daniel's discipline *does* cost him. His enemies watch his window to catch him in the act. And despite King Darius's distress when he learns of Daniel's fate (and realizes he's been hoodwinked), he must keep his word. It's the law, and not even the king can change it.

Daniel gets thrown into the lions' den.

In most situations, that would be it. We use the word "martyr" to describe someone who dies for the sake of Jesus. Only a few earn such a high honor and experience such grace.

But Daniel experienced a different outcome.

As soon as the sun rose the next morning, the king rushed back to the lions' den to see what had become of Daniel. A tormented Darius hadn't slept all night and had eaten nothing. We pick up the story in Daniel 6:

> At the first light of dawn, the king got up and hurried to the lions' den. When he came near the den, he called to Daniel in an anguished voice, "Daniel, servant of the living God, has your God, whom you serve continually, been able to rescue you from the lions?"
> Daniel answered, "May the king live forever! My God sent his angel, and he shut the mouths of the lions. They have

not hurt me, because I was found innocent in his sight. Nor have I ever done any wrong before you, Your Majesty."

The king was overjoyed and gave orders to lift Daniel out of the den. And when Daniel was lifted from the den, no wound was found on him, because he had trusted in his God.[14]

Fascinating, isn't it? But it shouldn't be all that surprising. This is who our God is. And while he doesn't always choose to rescue his people from death (Example A: Jesus), he does promise to be with them through everything.

Time and again, we find that the disciplined possess the strength to endure life's greatest sufferings.

How crucial was Daniel's devotion to his deliverance? Did it make a difference? Perhaps not in the outcome (God's sovereignty surely outweighs our desire), but I wholeheartedly believe it made a profound impact when the king's men sealed the entrance to the den.

This is the beauty of discipline. Over time, the rhythms and practices we develop in spending time in the Lord's presence deepen the wells of intimate relationship with him.

Zealous People of Discipline

Martyrs tend to be zealous people of discipline. Their passion for God matches or even exceeds their devotion to him. When times get difficult, they press in. When adversity strikes, they run to Jesus.

Gerald L. Sittser beautifully illustrates this concept in his book, *Water from a Deep Well*. In his chapter on martyrdom, he presents a story about a young girl named Perpetua, forced to make a difficult choice.

As a wealthy, young, influential wife and mother, Vibia Perpetua (AD 181–203) was arrested for converting to Christianity. In a vision, she learned that she'd soon die if she didn't recant her allegiance to Jesus. Her father pleaded with her to change her mind, even guilting her with the life of suffering to which she'd commit her newborn baby.[15]

Perpetua refused to recant. "I am a Christian," she kept repeating.[16]

Sittser puts her decision into proper perspective:

> For the sake of Christ she happily submitted to death. She made a decision, not between life and death but between Christ and Rome. Her courage and determination only reminded them that perhaps there was more to these Christians than meets the eye. Could it be that what they believed was actually true? If so, then the state itself would have to face a competition that it had never had to face before.[17]

Live rich, secure, and with a family? Or die alone as a Christian?

Perpetua chose the latter.

Where did she find such devotion? It all stemmed from her discipline.[18]

We find the same thing with Daniel—and it can be so with us as well. Discipline cultivates relational intimacy.

We know this, don't we?

My wife feels loved, seen, and known when we partake in the weekly discipline of a date night.

Our community feels loved, seen, and known when we discipline ourselves to gather around the table weekly.

Our church feels loved, seen, and known when we choose to show up to our Sunday morning gathering.

These relational disciplines lead to relational depth. Why would we think it's any different with God? But we do. So, we imagine:

If you truly love God, you won't need to set an alarm; you'll just wake up.

If you truly love God, you'll just know what to pray.

If you truly love God, then you'll just let the Spirit guide you.

Do you see the consequences of laziness at work here? Now, please don't mishear me. I'm not discrediting the work and power of the Holy Spirit. I believe that whenever God wants to do so, he can move us to action from inaction.

I just don't think that's the way he most *wants* to relate to us.

Remember the half-court shot? Will it go in? Maybe once or twice if you're a novice. Maybe every now and then if you occasionally practice. But if you discipline yourself to master that shot, eventually it will start to fall with greater frequency (looking at you, Steph Curry).

Disciplining yourself to spend time in the presence of the Lord will increase your ability to discern and discover the Holy Spirit at work.

You're not a bad Christian for scheduling time and disciplining yourself to be with God. To the contrary, you're a great partner.

In the same way that faithful, committed spouses carve out intentional time together, so too should the bride of Christ—the church, us—carve out time to spend with Jesus.

Learning from Desert Fathers and Mothers

The Desert Fathers and Mothers figured this out a long time ago. We'd be wise to learn from their ways. How's the saying go?

If it ain't broke, don't fix it.

Yeah, that applies here.[19]

Around the third century after Jesus ascended to heaven, the Desert Fathers and Mothers retreated to solitary places to form monastic communities. Within those communities, they developed a practice drawn directly from Jesus' teaching in John 15 (more on that in a moment). They called their practice "A Rule of Life."

Many years later, St. Augustine and St. Benedict, two "church fathers" (or what I like to call "legends," powerfully influential people in the faith), popularized the practice by writing, sharing, and observing their own Rule of Life. They cultivated communities centered around three key elements: prayer, study, and work.

I know, I know—heady stuff.

"So what?" you might ask. "Why would I want to follow Jesus if my relationship to him gets reduced to a set of rules? Isn't that the opposite of what Jesus taught?"

Yes, it is.

We know the phrase: Jesus isn't nearly so concerned with rules as he is with relationship.

While that's true, we find the key here in the language used. Notice this practice is called a *Rule* of Life, not *Rule(s)* for Life. The nuance is subtle, the contrast stark.

We derive our English word "rule" from the Latin root, *regula*, which means either "a straight piece of wood" or "a ruler." We get the metric tool's name from it. A rule is a fixed entity: steady, sturdy, and straight.

In a world where we center our aspirations on achieving (through goals, benchmarks, analytics, and resolutions), a Rule of Life focuses on who we are *becoming*. When we center ourselves in that way, we find Jesus. It's an inside-out rather than a downside-up lifestyle.

Author and Benedictine scholar, Esther de Waal, writes, "*regula*, a feminine noun, carries gentle connotations: a signpost, a railing, something that gives me support as I move forward in my search for God."[20]

While the etymology of *regula* remains a topic of debate, most scholars believe the most accurate English translation is "a trellis." A trellis is a tool used to hold up a plant or a vine to aid its growth. Without a trellis, the vine either lacks depth and height (two key factors of health), or it withers under the poor, ground-level environment where natural predators or harsh environmental factors can destroy it.

In the same way, without a rule, a *regula*, or a trellis to uphold our spiritual growth, we make ourselves vulnerable to many similar dangers. So, while the word "rule" may scare you off, I invite you to give the practice a chance.

And in fact, *you're already practicing it* without knowing that you are. We all live our lives either with or without intention. Should you choose to bypass this exercise, you will still participate.

Or in other words, you will either live your life or your life will live you. A passive way of life is still a way of life.

Two Suggestions

This Rule of Life derives from Jesus' teaching in John 15: "I am the vine; you are the branches. If you remain in me and I in you, you will bear much fruit; apart from me you can do nothing."[21]

A Rule of Life seeks to develop and stake a trellis for the Vine to dwell on, so that life-giving fruit may spring up in abundance. If practiced intentionally, I believe a Rule of Life can revolutionize the way you follow Jesus. Through it, you can set in motion purposeful, concrete rhythms to enrich your daily life.

For a Rule of Life to take deep root in your soul, I suggest the following:

1. Begin by sitting in Jesus' presence.

When we develop and implement practices and rhythms, we tend to lean toward an automatic creation of a to-do list. But don't let it become an obligatory, rigid, legalistic agenda. Helpful rhythms and practices develop out of a deep well of conviction for the type of apprentice and disciple of Jesus you believe God is calling you to be.

Once you've gained clarity on these desires and values, run them through the filter of spiritual rhythms.

Jesus himself practiced these rhythms, deeming them necessary to a life of abiding. They include but are not limited to:

- solitude and silence
- Scripture reading
- prayer
- fasting
- Sabbath
- community
- confession
- simplicity
- tithing
- honoring the body
- hospitality
- forgiveness

The point is not to incorporate every rhythm to the greatest degree but to lean into the practices you believe God is most calling you to practice during this season.

A Rule of Life, while fixed in nature, is fluid in motion. In fact, many experts[22] recommend reviewing your Rule every six months, if not more, to ensure that the rhythms you're practicing fit best with who God is calling you to become.

I love this aspect of a Rule of Life because it reminds me of the enormous pleasure of following a Savior who generates joyful agents of abiding, not slaves of repetition. I revise my Rule of Life once a quarter to fit my varying seasons of life.

2. Sort out at what pace you will practice your rhythms.
Once you've sorted out the necessary rhythms and practices for your life, the time comes to sort out at what pace you will practice these rhythms.

Most Rules, but not all, categorize their practices into daily, weekly, monthly, quarterly, and annual habits. See these time categories not as barriers but as edges to your trellis. They help make up, from bottom to top, the structure needed to ensure a strong foundation.

If you're type A, like me, you may find this super helpful. If you're not, then don't feel as if you need to tie yourself down to timelines. Crafting a consistent rhythm will help regardless of how you choose to do it. I've put together a free ebook, *A Guide to Crafting a Rule of Life*, that you can access via my website as a resource to help you in this practice.[23]

Don't Take any Shortcuts

As you step onto the trail God's called you to blaze, many times will come when you'll feel tempted to get lazy. You'll feel like taking the easy route, the shortcut, or giving up altogether.

In those moments, God extends to you an invitation to lean in and press on. Remember that discipline today drives devotion tomorrow. Every decision you make amounts to a slow build toward who you become.

Jesus modeled for us daily faithfulness. He calls us to become like him and to live into our God-given purpose.

You have what it takes.

9

UNCOMPLICATE LIFE, GAIN SUBSTANCE

Simplicity

"THIS IS THE MOST BEAUTIFUL BUILDING I've ever seen."

I could hardly contain my excitement as I scrolled through Google images after Thanksgiving dinner.

"What is that?" Rylei asked.

"It's a Cistercian monastery."

"A what?"

"A certain type of monk's sanctuary."

Rylei immediately lost interest. But before you do, too, hear me out.

I had just finished reading Esther de Waal's *The Way of Simplicity*.[1]

She does a masterful job of breaking down and explaining the Cistercian way. Here's one of many incredible excerpts:

> In a Cistercian building we find a "subdued and bare art."[2] Here is simplicity, in the use of authentic materials, the careful blending of light and shade, the emphasis on sobriety of line. Here there is nothing superfluous that might distract the mind from God. This austere beauty, without decoration, fancy sculpture or stained glass, has a calming, almost a purifying effect, which seems to throw us back on ourselves, and on God.[3]

These monks committed themselves to unleashing the beauty of simplicity. Their high value for it showed internally through their spiritual lives but also externally in their architecture.

Do yourself a favor and google it yourself (after you finish this chapter, of course).

Many of us are unfamiliar with the term "simplicity." We know about minimalism; it's all the rage (or, at least it was in 2010).

What is it now? "Clean aesthetics"? A "vibe"? You know what I mean: clean lines, muted colors, high quality.

But before it was a cultural shtick, simplicity was a spiritual practice.

And before Jesus modeled for us the way of simplicity, the man who blazed the trail for Jesus himself modeled it for us.

Say "hi" to John the Baptist.

A Sudden Appearance

All four of the Gospels describe part of John the Baptist's story. The man makes a rather sudden appearance. Consider Luke 3:

> In the fifteenth year of the reign of Tiberius Caesar—when Pontius Pilate was governor of Judea, Herod tetrarch of

Galilee, his brother Philip tetrarch of Iturea and Traconitis, and Lysanias tetrarch of Abilene—during the high-priesthood of Annas and Caiaphas, the word of God came to John son of Zechariah in the wilderness.[4]

The next thing we know, three of the Gospels tell us that John immediately began preaching "a baptism of repentance for the forgiveness of sins."[5] People flocked to him by the hundreds, receiving correction, turning from sin, and getting baptized and ushered into a new way of life.

Eventually, even Jesus steps into the scene. John baptizes him too.[6]

What about this man allowed him to obtain such widespread influence?

Simple. John had a laser focus on fulfilling the call God had placed on his life. John had a trail to blaze, and he would let nothing deter him from accomplishing his assignment.

The Bible doesn't write a ton about John the Baptist, but from the small excerpts that focus on him, we see *simplicity* as one of his central values. In fact, I'd argue that John manifests simplicity in three key areas:

Simplicity in possessions.

Simplicity in persona.

Simplicity in purpose.

We need only a handful of verses in the Gospels to unpack each one.

1. Possessions

Mark tells us "John wore clothing made of camel's hair, with a leather belt around his waist."[7] The leather belt marked John out as, at best, a working-class citizen. The belt offered John the option of tucking in his tunic, providing greater freedom of movement for the labor he carried out to survive.

Also, not on anyone's list of costly clothing choices: camel hair. Historian and author Elizabeth Fletcher writes,

> Then as now, clothes—the right sort—let rich people show they were wealthy. Rich people had: clothes for winter and summer, clothes for going out and staying at home, or for work and leisure, and clothes of different materials—fine linen, fine wool, or sometimes in the later period, silk.[8]

John's diet also offers us some insight into his tax bracket: "He ate locusts and wild honey."[9]

Not quite the *Whole Foods* diet.

But that's the point. John had very few possessions and needed little to survive. His clothing choices and eating habits directly reflected the unglamorous lifestyle he'd chosen.

2. Persona

A more descriptive word here may be "lifestyle" (but, let's be honest, you'll remember this much easier if it's alliterated). From the very beginning, John had a very simple persona or lifestyle.

In Luke 1, John's father, Zechariah, receives a vision of the birth of his son and gets instructions:

> An angel of the Lord appeared to him, standing at the right side of the altar of incense. When Zechariah saw him, he was startled and was gripped with fear. But the angel said to him: "Do not be afraid, Zechariah; your prayer has been heard. Your wife Elizabeth will bear you a son, and you are to call him John. He will be a joy and delight to you, and many will rejoice because of his birth, for he will be great in the sight of the Lord. *He is never to take wine or other fermented drink*, and he will be filled with the Holy Spirit even before he is born."[10]

The angel instructs Zechariah to consecrate (or set apart) his son, John. Zechariah understood that John's forsaking of wine or fermented drink included a larger commitment called the Nazirite vow (mentioned in chapter 2). Someone taking a Nazirite vow abstained from alcohol, avoided touching dead bodies, and refrained from cutting his hair.

And why does this matter? Because Luke 1 says,

> And the child grew and became strong in spirit; and he lived in the wilderness until he appeared publicly to Israel.[11]

John's lifestyle crafted his persona. He led a simple life, a reclusive, solitary life in the wilderness. His refusal to consume alcohol, touch corpses, or cut his hair would've given him a wild appearance. No one would have missed his extremely simple lifestyle, appearance, and persona, especially once he appeared publicly.

And all of this led up to the singular purpose God had given him.

3. Purpose

Matthew 3 describes for us John's purpose:

> This is he who was spoken of through the prophet Isaiah:

> "A voice of one calling in the wilderness,
> 'Prepare the way for the Lord,
>   make straight paths for him.'"[12]

An angel had placed this assignment on John even before his birth.[13] Zechariah remembered it like this:

> And you, my child, will be called a prophet of the Most High;
>   for you will go on before the Lord to prepare the way for him,
> to give his people the knowledge of salvation
>   through the forgiveness of their sins.[14]

Surely, John's parents spoke this calling over him constantly. Why else would John, after thirty years in seclusion, immediately begin fulfilling the prophecy? John knew he had a trail to blaze, and nothing would stop him.

After Jesus began his public ministry and people stopped flocking to John and instead flocked to Jesus to be baptized, that simple purpose remained clearly in focus. John himself declared,

> You yourselves can testify that I said, "I am not the Messiah but am sent ahead of him." The bride belongs to the bridegroom. The friend who attends the bridegroom waits and listens for him, and is full of joy when he hears the bridegroom's voice. That joy is mine, and it is now complete. He must become greater; I must become less.[15]

John's simplicity in possessions, persona, and purpose help us to see how combatively he opposed the temptation to pursue status.

Anyone in John's position—publicly popular after thirty years in seclusion—would feel either honored or overwhelmed by the sudden attention. Eventually, such success can become a source of real temptation:

"I'm pretty good at this."

"A lot of people are getting saved through me."

"My name is getting out there. This is cool!"

The motivation for increased status, fame, popularity, or even love can, as it often does, begin to grow. Our flesh craves the attention, affirmation, and acceptance that come with success. To deny this is to deny our human nature. We want to be known and loved. The more people who profess their love and acceptance for us, the more important we feel.

And yet, John's simple life culminated in an extraordinarily counter-cultural status statement: "He [Jesus] must become greater; I must become less."[16]

That's beautiful simplicity at work. But is it possible for us to replicate? Must we cease caring for our appearance, eating great food, or ambitiously achieving good work?

I don't believe so.

Developing simplicity of heart, however, can go a long way toward preventing a focus on status from overtaking our ego.

Moving Toward Simplicity

Richard Foster writes, "Simplicity is an inward reality that can be seen in an outward lifestyle. We must have both; to neglect either end of this tension is disastrous."[17]

John the Baptist is our archetype for holding these two realities in perfect tension. His inward posture ("He must become greater, I must become less") and his outward lifestyle (simple dress, appearance, and diet) all enabled him to live in faithful obedience and allegiance to Jesus.

So, why not follow his lead?

How can we develop simple lives regarding our possessions, persona, and purpose? That discovery may lead to a reality-altering shift that allows us to further embrace the trail God's called us to blaze.

1. Possessions

America, and the developed world in general, provides a case study in a lack of simplicity. We've bought into the consumeristic lie that "more money = more happiness." We've heard it a million times, we know it's not true, and yet . . . our hoarding of possessions belies our professed belief.

We consume more material goods, have bigger homes, and own more items on average than any humans at any other point in history.[18] In fact, 10 percent of the US population doesn't even have enough space to hold its stuff. Did you know that over the past forty years, the self-storage business has been the fastest growing segment of the commercial real estate industry?[19] We're trending the wrong way with respect to owning less.

And why does it matter? It's just stuff, isn't it?

If only that were true.

Jesus wasn't messing around when he said, "Where your treasure is, there your heart will be also."[20] More stuff means more things to care about, be responsible for, and take care of. At some point, our stuff becomes a hindrance, not a help.

Rylei loves watching the horrid TLC show, *Hoarders: Buried Alive*. More than anything, it just makes me sad for those individuals. We witness in real time people who have become slaves to stuff.

Surely, there must be a better way?

I believe the way of Jesus says, "Simplicity is the answer."

Call it by whatever term you prefer—frugality, minimalism, simplicity—the answer is the same. I love Joshua Becker's definition, even if I don't prefer his term: "Minimalism: the intentional promotion of the things we most value and the removal of anything that distracts us from them."[21]

Sounds like a page taken out of John the Baptist's journal.

Really, how much of our stuff just sits around, wasted and useless? We have things called "junk drawers" . . . and that's *normal*?

What if we were to become more intentional with our material possessions? What if we began to take inventory of the clothes we wore, the food we ingested, and the things we buy? Before you write me off, I don't see this as idealistic. I believe it's *wise*.

I'm not talking about a legalistic list of "have to's," I'm talking about a biblically sound way of life. Consider just one of many examples Scripture gives us regarding simplicity:

But godliness with contentment is great gain. For we brought nothing into the world, and we can take nothing out of it.[22]

Since you can't take it with you, why store up treasures on earth that will soon wither and turn to dust?

Before we move on, let's get practical. If you're looking to lean into simplicity, try these:

CONSCIOUS SHOPPING

It would probably horrify most of us to know the unethical processes that went into creating most of our fashion wear. What we see as a simple score at the mall cost a fourteen-year-old in Burma twelve hours to make, at far less than the minimum living wage.[23] That's not a slam on you, but it should raise an eyebrow.

When you buy clothes, try a site like Good On You to determine how sustainable and ethical your clothing is.[24]

When you buy food, go local as often as possible.

If you buy electronics, shoes, or other household items, use the 1:1 rule: if something comes in, something else goes out. I'm relentless on this. This rule helps ensure that our house doesn't get overly cluttered.

QUALITY OVER QUANTITY, ALWAYS

I used to be the "deal king." I would walk into outlet malls, retail stores, and other suppliers and walk out with hundreds of dollars' worth of items for a fraction of the cost. I used to pride myself on it: "Look at how much I got for such a little price!"

But so many times, most of the items went unused or unworn. Years later, they'd end up in a Goodwill pile. What a destructive, wasteful cycle!

I finally decided to buy only what I needed, when I needed it, ensuring that its good quality would make it last. Before you scoff at high-end purchases, think about it: What will last longer? One $200 well-made jacket? Or three $70 jackets made of inferior materials that you got on the sale rack for forty bucks each because of a design/material error? Many reasonable retailers provide high quality, made-to-last clothing that won't break the bank.

(Note: I know how pretentious an exercise like this can seem: "Hey, must be nice to buy a $200 jacket. I can afford to shop only at Walmart or Goodwill." I get it. Truly. But no matter where you shop, I'd like to gently encourage you to ask, "How often will I wear this? Is it worth the real price that it cost to make?")

The point? Purchase wisely, consciously, and intentionally.

PURGE

Take a day to go through your closet, your kitchen, your office, your garage, or your whole home (if you're feeling ambitious), and purge any unnecessary items. Pull it all out and ask, "Do I *really* need this?" If you don't, sell it, donate it, or throw it away.

Purge with the mindset that you are not "making room" for more stuff, but that you're simplifying your life to contain less stuff.

What would it look like for you to live in a space where everything had a purpose? Where each possession had a use? How much less stress would you feel after cutting in half the amount of stuff you must care for? How much more generous could you be once you realized the value of living with less?

When you discover the value of owning less stuff, you begin to cultivate a lifestyle of simplicity that adds layers of good to the world around you.

2. Persona

As you begin to live with less, you start to become a simple person (I mean that in the most positive sense).

Think about the most godly person you know. I would guess (a big assumption) that they don't own much. And they probably haven't owned much for a while. Or, I bet they live with an immense amount of tactile stability. Meaning—their possessions have stayed consistent over the years.

I'll give you an example . . .

The godliest person I know is my spiritual director. Every time she welcomes me into her home, I immediately sense a familiarity with my surroundings. Just inside sits the same shoe rack with the same shoes that she and her husband wear every day. We go into the same room every session and sit on the same couch that overlooks the same field with the same horses grazing.

It's simple. Familiar. Stable.

My spiritual director and her husband have forsaken the desire for more. They feel content with where they are and with who they are—and it *shows*. When you practice simplicity, your persona and lifestyle also become simple.

To clarify, they have a large home filled with items. Simplicity need not mean scarcity! They're well into their old age and have accumulated a lifetime's worth of stuff. But whatever they do own, they own on purpose. *Everything* has a purpose. It's tasteful.

The coffee table in her room houses the same candles and matches that she lights before every session. It's practical. It's functional. It gets used.

My spiritual director and her husband are beautiful people, but they're weathered. No Botox or steroids keep their age at bay. Very little makeup or trendy clothing (if any) camouflage their aging bodies. And yet they are *irresistible*. Within them lies a peace, a strength, a security, and a confidence that I long to have.

And yet, I often attempt to find such peace, strength, security, and confidence in my possessions, accomplishments, or platform.

Why?

Paul's words ring true here: "Godliness with contentment is great gain."[25]

When we learn to live with less, we spend less time trying to appear as more than we are. In the place of materialism, selfish ambition, striving for success, promotion, platforms, or praise, we begin to cultivate what Paul calls the "fruit of the Spirit": "The fruit of the Spirit is love, joy, peace, forbearance, kindness, goodness, faithfulness, gentleness and self-control. Against such things there is no law."[26]

So, is it wrong to dress up? To wear makeup? To look well-dressed?

Of course not. Please, don't misunderstand me. While none of those things are inherently wrong, if we prioritize them above our own inward formation, we—as author Richard Foster says—invite disaster.

To develop a simple lifestyle and to adopt a simple persona is to place Jesus at the center. Thomas Kelly puts it this way:

Life from the Center is a life of unhurried peace and power. It is simple. It is serene. It is amazing. It is triumphant. It is radiant. It takes no time, but it occupies all our time. And it makes our life programs new and overcoming.[27]

I want to live a life that matters.

As I simplify my possessions and adopt a simple persona, I free myself to seize the God-given purpose graciously given to me.

3. Purpose

We all want to live a life that matters. I presume that's why you're reading this book.

But how often do we grow distracted with respect to living a life that matters? To grow deep roots, make a real difference in a specific community, to stay, to remain committed—none of that is celebrated . . . at least, culturally speaking.

To make a lasting change takes time. In a world of overnight success, instant fame, and digital idolatry, it's easy to get swept up in a wanderlust that longs for more. Our desire for status convinces us that to make the biggest difference means to affect the most people.

But consider this: we serve a Savior who most believe never traveled more than 100 miles away from his hometown. This fact flies in the face of what we deem as success.

We live in a world where professional athletes switch teams every year. Where business executives leave one company for a rival to earn a greater salary. Where families uproot and move to more effectively position their kids to get into the college of their choice.

Again, none of this is inherently wrong. But what's the heart posture behind such moves? Typically, it's more money, more success, or more fame—or at least, what we perceive as an *opportunity* for such things.

John the Baptist remained focused on a single mission throughout his life. God called him and set him apart for one thing, to make way for the King of kings and the Lord of lords.

Until Jesus was ready, John waited. When Jesus publicly announced his ministry, John surrendered any further upward mobility, saying, "He must become greater; I must become less."[28]

A Title to Envy

The great saints of this world have a title that I envy. Jesus does too.

Francis *of* Assisi.

Joan *of* Arc.

Athanasius *of* Alexandria.

Augustine *of* Hippo.

Cyprian *of* Carthage.

Teresa *of* Calcutta.

The names given to the great saints of our Christian heritage all have a simplistic nature. God called each of them to a place. A *singular* place. And they blazed the trail that only they could, making a profound impact on the individuals in their wake.

Their faithfulness, their character, their consistency, and their commitment created legacies that we still talk about today. But no more than the legacy of our Savior.

Jesus *of* Nazareth. Jesus *the Christ*.

And we shouldn't forget Jesus' forerunner:

John *the Baptist*.

Both men, named after a singular mission, given by God for them to fulfill.

Which brings us here . . .

What has God called *you* to?

What's the dream? The ache? The longing stirring inside you?

What trail has God called you to blaze?

Whatever it is, think big but think less.

You could do a million things; our modern world certainly doesn't skimp on possibilities. But no one can do a million things *well*.

What if you stepped onto the trail God asks you to blaze and just . . . stayed there? With no desire to glow up but instead to grow down? To root yourself in a singular mission and to commit your life to it?

I love to dream about being Micah *the Pastor*. Micah *the Writer*. Micah *of Indianapolis*.

With Jesus at the center, what has he called you to do?

What beauty could your paintings display forty years from now?

What depth could your poems reach based on decades of life lived?

What impact could you have on a single street from a single home, occupied over the course of a lifetime?

These questions eat at me in the best way. In an age when we equate purpose with importance, John flips it and equates purpose with obedience. To John, it's simple: do what God has called you to do.

What if the trail God's called you to blaze isn't long, but deep? You'll never know unless you become comfortable with a single, simple, slow burn.

10

LOVE (PERIOD)

Love

ONE SATURDAY SOME TIME AGO, Rylei and I ended up having one of *those* days. You know what I mean?

A day where it feels like *nothing* is going right? Yeah. It was one of those days.

Frankly, our troubles probably stemmed from our disobedience to the weekly rhythm we felt God had called us to keep. If you don't know, when God created everything,[1] he formed a pattern of work and rest. He created everything in six days: the universe, sun, moon and stars, the earth, the birds of the air, the fish of the sea, human beings, and everything in between.

And on the seventh day, God rested. He delighted. He stopped and simply enjoyed the result of his labor.

We call this the Sabbath or, "the day of rest."

To "shabbat" (or sabbath) literally means "to stop."[2] It's a day of rest from all forms of labor and all attempts at striving. On that day we uncouple from to-do lists and errands and expectations. We stop, make ourselves present, rest, and commune with one another and with God.

As practicing followers of Jesus, Rylei and I have tried to intentionally adhere to this rhythm of work and rest, work and rest, work and rest. We do so not to be legalistic, rule-following Christians, but because for us, a life of abiding in Jesus requires margin and space within our souls to re-center and reorient ourselves to God.

For us, the Sabbath manifests in the rhythm of every Friday night, shutting off our phones, lighting a candle, and relishing in twenty-four hours of exercises and activities that bring us life. We pick things that fill our souls to overflowing and attune us to being the loving, kind, present people of Jesus that he calls us to be.

We consider this day a gift that fills and carries us through the next six days.

The specific Sabbath I'm recalling was *not* one of those days. Rather than a beautiful picture, it turned into a nightmare.

Rylei and I had endured a crushing week that had left us empty and behind on things we needed to do. So, on Saturday morning, upon awaking, Rylei said that she wanted to go run some errands. I had a choice: push back and risk a potential fight or passively go along with her wicked ways . . . I'm kidding!

Nevertheless, I chose the path of least resistance. I said nothing and we ended up running all around town.

The day did not go as planned.

We missed stores, we forgot things, we had to deal with people as we checked out. By the end of the day, we both felt exhausted. On our way home from our grueling trek of the entire city of Indianapolis, we realized our dog had no food.

Since I didn't want a visit by animal control, I ran into Walmart, grabbed the biggest bag of dog food I could find, and despite carrying a forty-pound bag on my shoulder, I felt compelled to stand in an actual checkout line.

Do you remember those? The lines with real people, individuals at the store with whom you must speak?

That's where I ended up.

I felt rushed, hurried, and overwhelmed. I huffed and puffed, frustrated at how our Saturday had turned out. I felt tired, hungry, and ready just to be home.

When I'm feeling those things, I often engage in an easy practice. I do something that makes me wait.[3] On this particular Sabbath, I decided to stick it to the man (or my wife) and *wait* in a physical checkout line. Take *that*!

As I stood in line, I noticed in front of me a struggling single mom. She had a baby on her hip and another baby in the cart, both of them melting down. She looked like she could use a Sabbath (or 100 Sabbaths). I had just earned some extra money and I'd told Rylei I wanted to tithe on those earnings.

In that unrushed, present, calm, centered moment as I stood in line, I felt the Holy Spirit whisper to me, *Pay for her groceries.*

Have you ever had an internal wrestling match with the Holy Spirit? On that day, I was having none of it. I fired back, silently: *You pay for her groceries!* (Remember, internal wrestling match. No psychiatrists got called).

But I couldn't shake the feeling. Finally, I said (again silently), *Holy Spirit, if her bill is for less than $200, I'll buy her groceries.*

Now, I don't recommend this as a spiritual practice. Jesus says, "Do not put the Lord your God to the test."[4] But that day, I broke that rule.

Strike two on our botched Sabbath day.

I eventually came out of my wallowing to hear the voice of the clerk telling the single mother, "That'll be $198 please."

Naturally, I swept in, informed her that the Holy Spirit had instructed me to pay for her groceries, and I became the hero of the day.

Not quite. I wish the story had gone that way.

Instead, I'm embarrassed to confess that on this Sabbath—as an apprentice of Jesus—not only did I not listen to the Holy Spirit's prompting, but I bought into the lies running through my mind.

She's going to think you feel sorry for her.

You're going to embarrass her even more than she's probably already feeling.

Her ethnicity differed from my own and so in these divisive times, I also thought, *Everyone's going to think you're racially profiling her. Or she's going to feel threatened by you coming in and thinking that you can just pay for her groceries.*

By the time all these thoughts came and went, I had missed the opportunity. She swiped her food stamps credit card and walked out of the store.

I never saw her again.

I returned home that night and couldn't sleep. All night long, the question tormented me: *What does love cost?*

In that moment at the store, I had the chance to show the love of Jesus to a woman who desperately needed to know that:

She was seen.

She was enough.

She was worthy.

She was winning the mom-game.

She didn't have to feel the burden to provide for her two young
babies on her own.

In that moment, I had the chance to redeem a day of angst and
hurry and bitterness with a tender act of obedience. I had the
chance to change for the better the course of someone's day, to
invite heaven on earth . . . but it would cost me something. And I'm
not talking about $200.

What does love cost?

If we're going to blaze the trail that Jesus has positioned us on, we
must answer that question. Because without love, the flame within
our heart dies out.

Selfless acts become selfish gain.

Courageous care turns into coercive pleasure.

Tender kindness becomes twisted manipulation.

Without love, we are nothing.[5]

No one in the Scriptures embodies the transformative power of love
more than the apostle John. His story and wisdom will shake us to
our core, draw us face-to-face with our selfishness, and equip us
to move further, faster, down the trail God has called us to blaze as
people of love.

Not the Ideal Candidate

"Sons of thunder."[6] That's the name Jesus originally gave to John
and his brother, James. Not the ideal candidate to become a
sage on love, right? Something about their speech, mannerisms,
tempers, or ambition led to Jesus giving them this name.

Intense. Like a clap of thunder.

John, along with his brother James and the apostle Peter, made up Jesus' inner circle. Time and again we see these three men present for some of Jesus' most intimate experiences with heaven.[7]

As Jesus hung on the cross, the Savior entrusted to John the care of his mother, Mary.[8]

We encounter the full scope of John's transformation in his first epistle, written after a lifetime of transformative living. Some fifty years[9] after the crucifixion, resurrection, and ascension of Jesus, John writes these words: "My dear children, I write this to you so that you will not sin."[10] John writes his entire letter with this single goal in mind.

So, how do we become people who do not sin?

Is it even possible?

On earth, no. But that's not John's point.

He insists that, through the transforming love of Jesus, we can repent, be forgiven, and commit to living "in the light."[11]

And how does one live in the light? John answers,

> We know that we have come to know him if we keep his commands. Whoever says, "I know him," but does not do what he commands is a liar, and the truth is not in that person. But if anyone obeys his word, love for God is truly made complete in them. This is how we know we are in him: Whoever claims to live in him *must live as Jesus did.*[12]

Love for God is made complete when we live as Jesus did. In other words, obedience to Jesus stems from a love for Jesus. When we truly walk in love, we long to live according to the way of Jesus.

In another of John's books, Jesus tells a remarkable story:

I am the true vine, and my Father is the gardener. He cuts off every branch in me that bears no fruit, while every branch that does bear fruit he prunes so that it will be even more fruitful. You are already clean because of the word I have spoken to you. Remain in me, as I also remain in you. No branch can bear fruit by itself; it must remain in the vine. Neither can you bear fruit unless you remain in me.[13]

If you're not familiar with first-century agriculture, no harm, no foul. Essentially, Jesus means that the fruit is in the root.

To adopt the qualities of a Trailblazer—character, initiative, submission, loyalty, etc.— we must be willing to mirror our exemplar, the Template himself, Jesus Christ. And more than any other virtue, Jesus demonstrates to us perfect love.

To become like Jesus, we must spend time with him and practice what he preached.

We can trace the fruit of wisdom and insight that we receive from John in his first epistle back to experiences or encounters he himself had with Jesus.[14] The fruit is in the root, remember? In 1 John 2, for example, John writes:

Anyone who claims to be in the light but hates a brother or sister is still in the darkness. Anyone who loves their brother and sister lives in the light, and there is nothing in them to make them stumble. But anyone who hates a brother or sister is in the darkness and walks around in the darkness. They do not know where they are going, because the darkness has blinded them.[15]

John gleans this insight from words that Jesus preached, which John recorded in his own Gospel:

When Jesus spoke again to the people, he said, "I am the light of the world. Whoever follows me will never walk in darkness, but will have the light of life."[16]

In 1 John 3, John exhorts his readers to "love one another,"[17] directly referencing Jesus' instructions to him and the other disciples during their lesson on the Vine.[18] John tells his readers to not be surprised if the world hates them,[19] again pulling directly from Jesus' teaching in John 15:

> If the world hates you, keep in mind that it hated me first. If you belonged to the world, it would love you as its own. As it is, you do not belong to the world, but I have chosen you out of the world. That is why the world hates you.[20]

Finally, John closes his own teaching on love with these words:

> This is how we know what love is: Jesus Christ laid down his life for us. And we ought to lay down our lives for our brothers and sisters. If anyone has material possessions and sees a brother or sister in need but has no pity on them, how can the love of God be in that person? Dear children, let us not love with words or speech but with actions and in truth.[21]

Sound familiar?

If you know your Bible, these words ring of Jesus' teachings in John 10, where he calls himself the Good Shepherd who lays down his life for his sheep.[22] It also echoes Jesus' words from his teaching on the Vine:

> My command is this: Love each other as I have loved you. Greater love has no one than this: to lay down one's life for one's friends.[23]

Coincidence? Of course not.

Plagiarism? Not entirely. During his time on earth, Jesus constantly told John and the other disciples what love is all about.

But can we say that John was no quick study? In fact, selfishness constantly tormented John. Do you recall that he referred to himself as the "disciple whom Jesus loved"?[24] My totally-not-certain-nor-theologically-credible opinion? I think it reflects John's attitude:

I'm the favorite.

Or how about the time he and his brother James begged Jesus for spots #2 and #3 in his coming kingdom?[25]

Or when they had their mom make the same request for them?[26] Yeah, that happened.

We also can't forget that John explicitly states in *his own Gospel* that *he* was the first to reach the empty tomb of Jesus, not Peter[27] (just in case you wondered).

A serious case of selfishness seemed to drive this guy.

And yet, five decades later, we see John using the words of Jesus in his own exhortation for believers to love one another. This is a changed man, a man who had been *with Jesus*. This man took Jesus' teaching seriously and literally. He abided in the Vine and the fruit became obvious.

The same man who consistently struggled with selfishness later exhorted people to lay down their lives for one another.

A son of thunder became a person of love.

This all became possible through John's commitment and allegiance to Love himself—to Jesus Christ.

And that same invitation has been extended to us.

What Is True Love?

In college, I thought of myself as the king of life hacking.

Okay, that may be a bit of an exaggeration. I was, however, a voracious reader of lifehack.org. At the time, it just made sense that I could read myself into a better life. David Brooks famously said his motivation for writing is to "write his way into a better life."[28]

Yeah . . . that's essentially what I've graduated to. *Three Keys to Leveraging Your Introversion* seemed far easier to digest than developing the courage to leave my social comfort zone.

I wish the same could be said about love.

Wouldn't it be nice to have a three-step process to loving others? And isn't that the end goal? What did Jesus name as the greatest commandment? Something about love,[29] right?

> "Love the Lord your God with all your heart and with all your soul and with all your mind." This is the first and greatest commandment. And the second is like it: "Love your neighbor as yourself."[30]

Yup, that's the end goal. To become *like* Jesus. To become people of love.

But it's a *process*. One that we can develop and improve as we seek to abide in the Vine. John's story gives testimony to this. He picked up some wonderful insight along the way that can help us as we seek to blaze the trail God has laid out for us.

All of this hinges on understanding the truth that God *is* love. John built his entire transformation on this bedrock truth. In another letter, he writes, "Whoever does not love does not know God, because God is love."[31] Many of us find this a difficult starting place because we naturally tend to associate love exclusively with emotion.

You see a provocative profile picture. You swipe right.

He buys you a beer. You wake up in his bed.

True love.

But is that *really* true love?

Too often, we equate love with infatuation. But a surge of intense passion or attraction does not equate to *agape*—all-encompassing, unrelenting, unconditional, sacrificial love.

True love is different.

True love exists and endures independently of how we *feel* in a present moment. That's what makes love, love. This kind of love, *agape* love, is active and demonstrated through our actions, not our emotions.

True love loves when love doesn't seem like a viable option. True love commits when "like" quits.

The apostle Paul lays out what true love looks like in action:

> Love is patient and kind. Love is not jealous or boastful or proud or rude. It does not demand its own way. It is not irritable, and it keeps no record of being wronged. It does not rejoice about injustice but rejoices whenever the truth wins out. Love never gives up, never loses faith, is always hopeful, and endures through every circumstance.[32]

Do you see the *actions* taking place? The *decisions* made? Look at that list. It doesn't say, "Love *feels* patient and kind," does it? It doesn't say, "Love isn't jealous, boastful, or proud when the *feeling* is right" or "Love doesn't give up except on its really bad days."

No!

Love *never* gives up, *never* loses faith, is *always* hopeful, and endures through *every* circumstance! That's love. That's God.

Because God is love.

God doesn't tie his love to conditions, feelings, or circumstances. His love flows out of his very nature, out of his character, out of his very being and existence. That's just who he is.

God is love.

Understanding that God is love should move us toward compassion. It should push us outside the bounds of our comfort zone and move us toward living out love in action. How does John, the guy who in Mark 10 pleads his case to sit at the right hand of Jesus, become a man who ends up writing these words? "If anyone has material possessions and sees a brother or sister in need but has no pity on them, how can the love of God be in that person?"[33]

This is a mighty transformation. But what did love cost?

It cost *everything*.

It cost John, daily, obeying Jesus' command to "take up [your] cross and follow me."[34]

The battle rages right here. To step faithfully onto the trail that God calls us to blaze, we must lay down our own selfishness that seeks to rule us. And we must say "no" to a culture that exalts and idolizes selfish success.

"Get your money."

"Grow your brand."

"Build your platform."

"You do you."

"You're a boss."

"You're the GOAT."

I don't know about you, but I say all these things to myself in the mirror every morning. (Sarcasm, remember? It's okay to laugh.) But that is the lure of selfishness. Selfishness will convince you that your personal importance outweighs God's preeminence. Thankfully, we serve a kind God.

Jesus foreshadowed that John would be transformed, but this

transformation would not lead to "worldly" greatness, success, or fame. Rather, it led to eternal influence.

The difference? Suffering love replaced selfishness. Out of suffering love, a Trailblazer was born. John had a front row seat to suffering love in action. John witnessed God, who *is* Love, live.

John witnessed Jesus move toward the margins of society and step outside the boundaries of relational comfortability.

And yet, this doesn't explain what gave John the confidence to change. Wouldn't someone as selfish and ambitious as John feel disqualified and unworthy to drink the cup and be baptized with the baptism of Jesus? Where'd John's hope come from? It seems that John drew from Jesus' words spoken to Nicodemus: "God so loved the world that he gave his one and only Son, that whoever believes in him shall not perish but have eternal life."[35]

Just because Christian culture has turned this verse into a cliché doesn't mean that we should negate its importance. Do you see the implication?

God *so* loved the *world*.

God *so* loved *you*. And *me*. And *everyone else*. He loved the world so much that he gave up Jesus, his one and only Son, in exchange for our eternal salvation.

We don't deserve it, we haven't earned it, but he gave it. He gave himself, freely and without cost to us. No penalties, no repayments, no hoops to jump through, no loopholes.

When Jesus hung on that cross and said, "It is finished," and then conquered death, that was it. Our eternity purchased, bought, redeemed by the blood of Jesus, God's only begotten Son.

Do you know how much God loves you?

Like, really?

Your interpretation of God's love will either fuel or drain your desire to share that love with others. Your motivation to extinguish selfishness in your life and grow in suffering love will either increase or decrease depending on your pursuit of Jesus (or lack thereof).

Your capacity to love will match your capacity to receive love.

If you don't believe within your heart that Jesus Christ died for you and that he loves you, how can you go out and love others, much less your enemies?

Why else would Jesus have challenged us to love our neighbor *as ourselves*? That kind of strength and capacity can be born only out of a deep, soul-level conviction that you are loved, that you are chosen and set apart, and that the blood of our Savior, Jesus Christ, has redeemed your life so you can become the Trailblazer he's called you to be.

The Life You've Always Dreamed Of

You fired up yet? Ready to run through a brick wall? I hope so.

But maybe—just maybe—a selfish kind of fear still paralyzes you.

What if I mess up?

What if I pick the wrong trail?

What if I fail?

What if things go wrong?

What if I make the wrong choice?

What if I have regrets?

Those what-ifs can really bog us down, can't they? But what if we flipped it?

What if God is who he says he is?

What if you blaze the trail?

What if you make a difference?

What if you leave a legacy?

What if you maintain your character?

What if your personal integrity outgrows and outpaces your platform?

What then?

Perhaps we'd discover the life we've always dreamed of, a life of living confidently in the security and assurance of God's love.

Agape love. Suffering love.

John seemed to finally grasp that. His words from 1 John 4 seem to reveal the transformational work he underwent. And he invites us to surrender our selfish fear and to pick up our cross and follow Jesus.[36]

> This is how we know that we live in him and he in us: He has given us of his Spirit. And we have seen and testify that the Father has sent his Son to be the Savior of the world. If anyone acknowledges that Jesus is the Son of God, God lives in them and they in God. And so we know and rely on the love God has for us.
> God is love. Whoever lives in love lives in God, and God in them. This is how love is made complete among us so that we will have confidence on the day of judgment: In this world we are like Jesus. There is no fear in love. But perfect love drives out fear, because fear has to do with punishment. The one who fears is not made perfect in love.
> We love because he first loved us. Whoever claims to love God yet hates a brother or sister is a liar. For whoever does not love their brother and sister, whom they have seen, cannot love God, whom they have not seen. And he has

given us this command: Anyone who loves God must also love their brother and sister.[37]

To John, blazing a trail is worthless without love. In fact, love itself is the point. Why? Because Jesus is love.

So, if you're desperately searching for why in the world you're here on this earth, can I encourage you? The answer is found in Love. In Jesus, who commanded us to love God and to love our neighbor as ourselves. He insisted that everything else hangs on this.[38]

What if we allowed love to serve as the defining mark of our apprenticeship to Jesus?

I'd say we'd be off to a pretty good start in the purpose-filled pursuit of becoming a Trailblazer.

11

NEVER GIVE UP

Redemption

I'D BEEN LOOKING for the right moment to intervene.

The fight already had raged for more than twenty minutes. It was 9:00 p.m. and neither I nor my two younger brothers could sleep.

So, I started my nightly round: I began in Elijah's room to console him, then moved to Isaiah's room to hold him, and then to the top of the stairs to pray for it all to stop.

As my parents' screams grew louder, there came a moment when I couldn't take it anymore. When it felt as if the situation had escalated to its highest point, I made my move. Storming down the stairs in a fit of rage—as if to make it painfully obvious that my brothers were still awake—I ran into the kitchen with my hands over my ears and yelled, "SHUT UP! SHUT UP! SHUUUT UPPPPP!" as loud as I could.

With hot tears streaming down my face, I then returned to the top of the stairs, curled up, and started to cry. To be alone. To wish, hope, and pray for all of this to stop. To pray for different parents. For a different family. To be anywhere but *here*.

Many mornings, I woke up in my bed, not knowing how I got there. Looking back, I know my parents had scooped me up on the way to their bedroom.

For years, this was our reality, with no end in sight. But on October 16, 2005, everything came to a head. The worst day of my life.

We had returned home from Sunday service at the church my parents had planted three years earlier. Things looked up and to the right . . . on the outside. The church had grown from twelve attenders to seven hundred in three years. Other churches had begun to ask my dad to preach and to coach other pastors. He'd become the star he'd always dreamed of becoming.

But on the inside, our family was a wreck. My parents had grown tired. Tired from church planting, tired from hustling, tired from scraping by, and tired of fighting about it all.

On this Sunday afternoon, things seemed relatively normal. Church and the McDonald's drive-through for lunch. Mom couldn't cook and Dad wouldn't. So, we had a Happy Meal and put on a happy face to soothe all the tension.

Until we got home.

The next thing I knew, my mom started screaming at my dad. Only, this time it sounded different. I heard so much pain in her voice that I ran and hid behind the couch. A few moments later, I saw my dad walking outside with a pile of clothes under one arm and some dry cleaning draped over the other.

"Daddy, where are you going?"

"Daddy's leaving."

"To go where?"

The car door slammed shut and my dad drove off.

With my dad gone and my mom distraught, I didn't know what to do. So, I just started walking. Eventually, I ended up at the house of my neighbor, Tyler.

Tyler: "What's up?"

Me: "I think my parents are going to get a divorce."

Tyler: "That sucks. That happened to me a few years ago."

Me: "Okay."

After our brief, unhelpful conversation, we ended up sitting in silence for thirty minutes or so. When I returned home, a crowd of people had gathered in our living room. Elders, board members, extended family members, and other confidants surrounded and consoled my mom. As I sat in another room, I could only faintly pick up on the discussion. Snippets, really.

". . . moral failure."

"He's done . . . "

"Yes, with her . . . "

". . . I don't know where he is. He says he's quitting on the church, our family, and God."

"This is really bad . . ."

"How are we going to tell everyone?"

Before pastoral failure became a daily occurrence on our Twitter timelines, it played out much more subtly in public but did just as much damage privately. My father's biggest failure rocked our family, church, and broader community: an extramarital affair with my mother's best friend and children's director at our church.

In the first couple of days post-confession, we saw no remorse, no recourse, and no reconciliation. Just hurt, pain, and trauma.

Oh . . . and the biggest failure imaginable.

A Catalytic Reminder of Our Sin

Human beings naturally feel uncomfortable with failure. To fail can mean many things, including a lack of success, an omission, a cessation, or a falling short.[1]

Could failure prick the core of our identity because God made us in his image? Although molded by a perfect, complete, without-lack Creator, we rightly see ourselves as imperfect, inadequate, incomplete, and lacking in so many ways.

I see failure as a catalytic reminder of our sinful nature. And yet, failure has become a part of our reality.

Those who've learned to grasp this truth have, by and large, accomplished great things. Thomas Edison, Oprah, Michelle Obama, John F. Kennedy, Bill Gates, and Bruce Lee, for example, all developed wise and helpful insights regarding their approach to failure.[2] One of the gravest mistakes we make is to equate "failure" with "finished." Cancel culture epitomizes this error.

Now, before you throw this book down and toss it in your fire, please hear me: I don't, in any way, want to diminish the hurt, pain, or brokenness caused by many individuals who have been *justifiably* canceled. I'm simply making a cultural observation.

For many, failure seems final. Not, however, according to the Scriptures.

We must grasp this to develop the strength and endurance required to blaze the trail to which God has called us. I doubt that anyone embodies this reality better than Peter.

Cue the Stereotypes

Before becoming one of the world's greatest apostles, evangelists, and writers, Peter worked as a fisherman. (Cue every stereotype you can think of regarding fishermen.)

Fishermen had no formal education, flashed hot tempers, cussed a lot, and possessed an uncanny amount of bravery and courage developed over the time they'd spent on the open sea, battling Mother Nature. In short, they included some of the toughest dudes around.

Enter Peter.

Throughout the Scriptures, we witness Peter display many of these stereotypical qualities. His first encounter with Jesus, however, sheds some light on the hope and transformation that the Savior of the world offers to us all.

After his first encounter with Jesus, Peter suddenly realizes who Jesus really is and nearly shouts, "Go away from me, Lord; I am a sinful man!"[3] Does it almost seem as though Peter physically wears his failure? Do you see here the shroud of shame?

Peter clearly does not see himself as healthy. Did Peter just want to portray himself as humble? I doubt it. Humility accepts, it doesn't deflect. Humility invites, shame expels. And here, Peter tries to expel Jesus from his presence.

How Jesus responds provides the key to understanding the trajectory of the trail that God would call Peter to blaze. Jesus replies, "Don't be afraid; from now on, you will fish for people."[4]

Do you see it?

Jesus immediately began unwinding Peter's insecurity and rebuilding his true identity. He took Peter's inward sense of failure (sinful man) and reclaimed Peter's future (fisher of people).

This is the beauty of the God we serve.

No failure is final to him—but that doesn't mean we have no process of restoration to undergo.

Jesus once asked his disciples, after they'd spent years following him, "Who do people say the Son of Man is?"[5]

The disciples began tossing out answers: "Elijah." "John the Baptist." "Jeremiah." "One of the prophets."[6]

And then Jesus flipped the script: "But what about you? Who do *you* say I am?"[7]

A test! The moment had come. Would they be ready? Could Jesus entrust them to move from apprentice to apostle?

And then a man named Simon stepped up and said, "You are the Messiah, the Son of the living God."[8]

Bingo!

A delighted Jesus replied, "Blessed are you, Simon son of Jonah, for this was not revealed to you by flesh and blood, but by my Father in heaven. And I tell you that you are Peter, and on this rock I will build my church, and the gates of Hades will not overcome it."[9]

Peter had arrived! From insecure, ashamed fisherman, to the *rock* or *foundation* on which Jesus would build his church.

That's quite a trail to blaze, isn't it?

This feels like *the* moment. From here on out, Simon becomes Peter, and Peter will build Christ's church. Peter will blaze the trail!

Except, he doesn't. At least, not right away.

Many months after this conversation, the high priest had Jesus seized and arrested. Could this be Peter's chance? Maybe he'd swoop in, save Jesus, and establish his church!

But, no.

Peter, the rock, in his Lord's greatest time of need, disappeared, disowned, and denied Jesus three times.[10]

What happens when we fail? We tell ourselves, "Get up and try again." But do we? I know this may feel like an elementary question, but it matters.

As you look over the course of your life, what do you see? Has life become a series of failures, missed opportunities, and mistakes? Have you found yourself a long way off from the trail God originally called you to blaze?

Go back to your dream. Are you living into it? Have you boldly dared to step into it? Or has shame held you back? Time and time again in Scripture, we see these moments become catalysts in the lives of Trailblazers.

What if Peter hadn't denied Jesus? What if he'd overcome his fear? What if he had stood by Jesus' side?

Wrong questions.

We serve a God who bends, not breaks. And Peter's *response* to his failure mattered more than the failure itself.

Four Steps to Redemption

After a few days, the initial pain and shock of my dad's failure, betrayal, and consequent public separation from my mother began to subside. We were alone, abandoned to figure out everything by ourselves. For a few weeks, it felt as though we'd suffered a sudden death in the family. Without Dad around, we felt lost.

And then the phone rang.

My dad expressed a desire to see my brothers and me. A few hours later, we got dropped off at the end of the driveway of a house belonging to one of our church's elders. My dad had moved in with them, as he and my mom refused to speak to each other.

As I made that long walk up the driveway to the house, I thought long and hard about what I would say. I hurt, and I wanted to hurt him back. After some awkward pleasantries and small talk, I finally let it out.

"Dad?"

"Yeah, buddy?"

"I hate you. I hate you so much."

Ruthless vengeance coursed through my veins.

"I can't believe you would leave us," I continued. "You're a coward. And I don't need you. I hate you."

The depth of my father's failure had finally sunk in for both of us. We'd hit rock bottom.

After another few days, my parents began attending intensive counseling. After a few sessions, I began to join them. Over the course of the next six months and subsequent six years (now eighteen years and counting), together we walked the journey of true redemption.

To blaze a trail post-failure is possible, but it requires repentance, acceptance, forgiveness, and commitment.

1. Repentance

At some point, you must recognize and admit your failure. Remorse and sorrow must follow the pain your actions have caused. Only then, in your broken state, can God begin to piece you back together. We see this pattern with Peter right after his denial: "And he went outside and wept bitterly."[11] Peter's lack of faith, courage, and devotion to his Rabbi broke him.

I'll never forget the day my dad gave in to true repentance. He and my mom were separated by that point. This was when he decided to become a person of truth. He puts it best in their memoir:

> On Monday I came to the house to pick up the boys for school. Trisha [Mom] appeared in the doorway and asked me to come in. I was content with getting the boys to school late, because being invited into the house trumped getting them to school on time. She sat down on the couch and said to me, "I have to know everything. Are you telling me everything?"
>
> I said, "As far as that relationship, I've told you everything. But I have a lot more to tell you; I'm just not sure you want to know."
>
> Trisha looked at me and said, "I want to know everything."
>
> I asked the boys to wait upstairs and watch television until I came up to get them for school. It was just Trisha and I on the couch. I didn't want to hide anymore. I confessed to her what I had already confessed to Keith. I told her I was so ashamed that I had refused to admit to these things or get help. She was sobbing. I was heaving, I was crying so hard. "I haven't just been lying to you; I've been lying to myself, and *I want to be a person of truth*, even if you don't want to be married to me anymore."
>
> In an act of grace and mercy unlike anything I'd ever seen or experienced, Trisha wiped my tears away and said, *"Now we can begin again. Now we can start over."*[12]

This is why we call it a turning point. To repent means to turn around, to go the opposite direction.

In this moment my dad surrendered his old way of life. He put down the habitual lying, cheating, and manipulation and stepped into—for the first time—100 percent authenticity and transparency.

When we reach our lowest point, are we willing to succumb to the grief of our shortcoming and sit in the pain that we've caused? It's a difficult yet necessary first step to move forward.

2. Commitment

As you embrace who God has called you to be, you must also commit to live into the life to which he has called you. To be a Trailblazer means to live in a "set apart" way that enables you to walk through "the narrow gate,"[13] as Jesus calls it.

You pursue a life of cruciform love.

After denying Jesus three times, it would have surprised no one if Peter had stayed in a bitter and weeping posture. He'd screwed up, and badly. But he committed to get back on the trail Jesus had called him to blaze. We witness this change on the morning of Jesus' resurrection.

About thirty-six hours after his denial, Peter "got up and ran to the tomb."[14] After some women returned with the news of Jesus' empty tomb, all the disciples stayed where they had hidden themselves, perplexed and paralyzed by fear.

Except Peter.

In that moment, Peter seemed to reclaim his true identity. Once again, he was God's rock, the one on whose shoulders Christ would build his church. This looked like a turning point for Peter . . . until, again, it wasn't: "Bending over, he saw the strips of linen lying by themselves, and he went away, wondering to himself what had happened."[15]

After Jesus' resurrection, he recommissioned Peter in a powerful seaside exchange.[16] In the end, Peter committed to becoming the man of faith Jesus had called him to be. He chose, at least for a moment, to believe that Jesus might actually be who he claimed.

For my dad, commitment to truth came in that counseling session; but he still had loads of baggage to uncover. Over the course of months, my parents had good days and bad days in the counselor's office. Sometimes, my dad would readily give over his full heart. Other times, the shame he felt fought tooth and nail to keep his authentic self at bay.

Commitment never seems to be a one-step process. It's more like two steps forward, one step back. But both Peter and my dad chose to get back on the trail, as intermittent at times as their commitment seemed.

None of this happens without consequences, as we see in the next progression in the process of redemption.

3. Acceptance

The shroud of shame can easily make acceptance into the most common area of failure in redeeming a situation. In this stage you either accept the consequences of your decisions, learn from them and grow, or you reject them and continue to repeat the cycle of unhealth that got you here in the first place.

Here's the truth, my friend; redemption is possible on the other side of failure. My dad says it best: "Failure is not final."[17] Still, the road to recovering your trailblazing identity does not happen without consequences.

For Peter, the consequences of his disappearance came in an intense, forty-eight-hours-ish stretch of loneliness, fear, doubt, and worry. His best friends went into hiding, his Master had died, the body had (presumably) been stolen, and the Romans might come after him next. It felt like a living nightmare.

What might have happened to Peter had he stayed? We'll never know. But we do know that in his cowardice, he ended up on the run, fearing for his life. Not a great place to be! And it happened as a direct consequence of his denial.

For my dad, the consequences, though they may seem obvious, included separation from his wife and kids; the loss of a job, a church, the trust of hundreds of people, and communal respect; a stripping of ordination and spiritual authority; and the hurt inflicted on everyone involved.

Even though my dad repented and committed to redeeming his story, certain consequences remained. For three months, he lived apart from us. For years, he had to rebuild trust with my mom. Even to this day, the sin of his past has left a permanent scar that, in some ways, will remain for the rest of his life.

A person living with shame might read a sentence like that and cower. But the Trailblazer sees scars the same way Jesus did, as part of our resurrected power. In Jesus, we experience new life. While this means the eternal forgiveness and redemption of our sins, it doesn't mean the removal of our scars. For evidence of this, just look at Jesus:

> On the evening of that first day of the week, when the disciples were together, with the doors locked for fear of the Jewish leaders, Jesus came and stood among them and said, "Peace be with you!" After he said this, he showed them his hands and side. The disciples were overjoyed when they saw the Lord. . . .[18]
> A week later his disciples were in the house again, and Thomas was with them. Though the doors were locked, Jesus came and stood among them and said, "Peace be with you!" Then he said to Thomas, "Put your finger here; see my hands. Reach out your hand and put it into my side. Stop doubting and believe."[19]

A Trailblazer on the path to redemption doesn't see scars as disqualification but as documentation of the healing work of Jesus Christ. As Paul puts it, "Therefore, if anyone is in Christ, the new creation has come: The old has gone, the new is here!"[20]

My parents have turned a tragedy into an amazing testimony. Peter too. Neither my dad nor Peter allowed their biggest failure to deter their future. Rather, Jesus redeemed, restored, and secured their future.

He can do the same thing for you—so long as you recognize that the consequences resulting from your sin don't stick around to punish you but to purify you. In your humble state of brokenness, committed to becoming a new creature (under the care of consequences), you become ready to move into the last phase of redemption.

4. Forgiveness

To truly redeem a broken situation, you must reach a point where you can forgive yourself for the wrong you've committed. Other parties involved may or may not choose to forgive you (a part of the consequence portion of this journey). We must understand this. But their choice to forgive or not forgive is out of your hands. If you've done the work—repented, committed, and accepted the consequences—and you've proven, over time, that your inner person is being transformed, then the only obstacle in the way of redemption is *you*.

Forgiveness became an anchor point for my parents and their story. My mother had to make the difficult choice to forgive not only her husband but also her best friend. Both had betrayed her trust and hurt her beyond words. To give insight into that process, I turn to her own words:

> Forgiveness is choosing to grieve and acknowledge that you have been wounded. Forgiveness uses anger to fuel your willingness to deal with your wound, and brokenness bridges the chasm between anger and healing. Brokenness is a complete surrender to God and his way, and with brokenness comes healing.
>
> Here's what this looked like for me. My wound was not the affair but broken trust. With each move, I felt that Justin had broken my trust. Now with the affair, I had to grieve the loss of my marriage, my best friend, and my church family. I became angry and begged God to show me the path to healing. In God's amazing grace, what he asked was that I become broken before him and recognize my own need for his grace and forgiveness. When I lived with a posture of gratitude for Jesus and his work on the cross, it prepared my heart to forgive and experience healing.
>
> *This is what forgiveness looks like: grief that is mourned, which turns to anger, which causes you to choose brokenness instead of bitterness, which allows you to experience healing.*[21]

My father found the process of forgiveness both great and difficult. He had many, *many* layers of shame to work through. At every turn, he had to choose whether to run, hide, and avoid, or to succumb to the pain. He puts it this way:

> Our marriage in many ways was in recovery mode, and we were growing in our love for one another. But the daily pain of my decisions ate away at my heart. It affected my view of myself. It affected my relationship with my kids. It affected my relationship with God.
>
> I felt undeserving. I felt unworthy. I felt like I should be unloved.
>
> I remember standing in the kitchen one evening and breaking down in tears. I knew God and Trisha had forgiven me, but I couldn't forgive myself. Trisha said to me, "Grace is only grace if you accept it. I've worked so hard to extend it to you, and you aren't accepting it. I forgive you. I think it's time to forgive yourself."
>
> Those words were like water to my parched soul. I didn't think I could ever forgive myself.
>
> If I forgive myself, doesn't that mean I'm getting away with something?
>
> If I forgive myself, doesn't that make it seem like I'm not paying for what I've done?
>
> If I forgive myself, who will remind me of how much of a screwup I am?
>
> But these thoughts did not allow me to see myself as Abba's child. In God's eyes I was already forgiven. To live as if this weren't true prevented me from finding all of my identity in my relationship with God.[22]

Every day, we must make a choice about whose voice we will believe: the voice of Truth or the voice of the enemy?

You must become willing to forgive yourself. You must accept your true identity as an adopted son or daughter of the One True King. Only then can you fully clothe yourself in the redemptive purpose of your life.

A few days after Jesus' death, burial, and resurrection, the Lord appeared to Peter. This is the only recorded conversation we have between Peter and Jesus since Peter's tragic failure:

> "Simon son of John, do you love me more than these?"
> "Yes, Lord," he said, "you know that I love you."
> Jesus said, "Feed my lambs."
> Again Jesus said, "Simon son of John, do you love me?"
> He answered, "Yes, Lord, you know that I love you."
> Jesus said, "Take care of my sheep."
> The third time he said to him, "Simon son of John, do you love me?"
> Peter was hurt because Jesus asked him the third time, "Do you love me?" He said, "Lord, you know all things; you know that I love you."
> Jesus said, "Feed my sheep."[23]

I mean, you can't make this up.

Three times Peter denied Jesus, and three times Jesus asked Peter, "Do you love me?" John tells us Peter felt hurt because Jesus asked him the question three times. I wonder if Jesus wanted to drive home the fact that he had forgiven every denial, every abandonment Peter had committed. And the Lord did so, one statement of love at a time.

Notice that at each pass, Jesus reminded Peter of the character he was to form, the man he was to become, and the legacy he'd been called to leave. After making each of his three statements, Jesus reminded Peter of his trail to blaze: "Feed my sheep."

Redemption!

Peter became the rock of the church and started a massive world-wide movement that has reached us today.

How?

He responded to the greatest failure of his life by accepting his true identity as a chosen, forgiven, redeemed son of God. Out of the depth of that failure came a triumphant life of trailblazing.

The Need for Perseverance

In the stories of Peter and my parents, we see yet another essential quality in the life of a Trailblazer: perseverance. The refusal to give up. To try again after failure. To overcome the shame and live into a true, pure identity in Christ.

Failure isn't final. It wasn't in Peter's story. It wasn't in my dad's story. And it doesn't have to be in your story. But you must be willing to trudge through the dark night and endure until the dawn comes.

Failure does not have to define the narrative of your story.

I write these words on Good Friday, the day the entire ancient world thought Jesus had failed. On that day, people laughed at, mocked, and made fun of this supposed "Savior" who claimed to be the Son of God. They all saw him as a fraud. A fake. A *failure*. Another religious fanatic to quickly forget.

But we know that's not the end of the story! Redemption comes in the morning.

So, too, with your story and my story. We are children of the Light. Redeemed, restored, and made whole by the blood of the slain and resurrected Lamb.

Don't give in to the shroud of shame. Have faith in the redemptive love of Jesus. You can reclaim, recover, and restore your dream if you choose to believe in and live out who God has called you to be.

Allow yesterday to fade into the past. Embrace the opportunity before you today. Believe that tomorrow will be different.

Your purpose awaits. The living water of Jesus is available. Show up to receive it again and again.

And again.

12

LEAN INTO BACKWARDS AMBITION
Quiet

WHILE ON A PLANE traveling back home to Indianapolis from Portland, Oregon, it finally clicked for me.

For months, I'd wrestled with what I considered a "missing piece" to the Trailblazer puzzle. In this cultural moment, what character trait would be the separator? The catalyst? The change agent for living a life like no one else?

I'd just finished reading an entertaining but troubling article about some of the ridiculous things people do to achieve Internet fame.[1] From drinking the contents of a snow globe, to breaking legs for the perfect pose, to Gorilla-gluing hair, creativity (and its harmful consequences) took center stage.

But the article did get me thinking: Had the lust for fame derailed any of the Trailblazers we've studied so far?

Ah, fame—the word has a nice ring to it. Oh, to be rich and famous! That's the goal, right?

Secure the bag.

Get your money.

Grow your clout.

Be an influencer.

But do we get authentic influence when we pursue it for inauthentic gain? Questions like these ran through my head on that plane ride from Portland to Indy in July of 2021.

The Seduction of Fame

The seduction of fame certainly has shown up in my own life.

By the time I was a seventh grader in 2010, Facebook already had established itself and Instagram and Twitter had begun to take off. The impetus of image began to consume me. The "like" button provided a high of affirmation that I'd never experienced.

Nowadays, we know that feeling comes from a chemical called dopamine coursing through our veins. Tons of research has shown how social media manipulates us, both chemically and biologically. People way smarter than me can explain it better.[2]

The point is, I was *hooked*.

As a fourteen-year-old, I had four times the number of social media followers than I do at the time of this writing, most of them *fake*. Yes, I admit it: I paid for followers (I can feel your judgment seeping through the page, okay?). I paid for praise, lusted for likes, and reached for relationships *at any cost*.

The epitome of insecurity.

But underneath all of that? I had an innate, human, healthy desire to be *known*. To be celebrated. To be accepted. To be liked.

To be *loved*.

For the next eight years, I went on a roller-coaster ride of love and hate with technology. For most of high school, I found my identity in social media. I incessantly checked my phone every time I received a notification that someone (or a "bot"[3]) *liked* a picture. On a good day I saw over 250 notifications come through my phone.

I had *arrived*.

But soon, I started to feel the growing discontent within my soul. To keep up my public persona took work, and a lot of it.

Why?

Because who I pretended to be in public didn't match who I was becoming in private.

Eventually, it all broke me. In 2015, I decided the time had come to make a change. Not only did I disable my social media accounts, I deleted them.

Sort of.

My retreat didn't last long. In 2016, I jumped back into the world of social media, albeit hesitantly. Soon, I fell back into finding status, identity, and prestige in my online persona.

So, in 2019, I decided to spend the entire year off of social media.

When I returned in 2020, I did so with a much more intentional frame of mind. I saw social media as a tool to use rather than as an avenue to achieve fame. Over the last few years, it's become nothing more than that: a place to share messages of hope and encouragement, to stay connected to a close circle of friends, and to reach the lost with the gospel.

And frankly? Putting social media in its place liberated me.

Now, I know this all has the potential to make me look like *that* guy. The guy who tells you to throw your iPhone in the water, to get a flip phone, and to go off-grid forever. But that's not the idea at all.

While I consider myself a digital minimalist, I am so by *conviction* and by *choice*. I know that to wade fully into the social media ocean makes me liable to the seduction of fame. Too easily I can become entranced by the idea of manipulating and exploiting social media as a weapon for personal gain, fame, and advancement.

This may sound overdramatic, but I think research backs me up in suggesting that our relationship to social media and technology at large can literally mean life or death.[4] I know that my story may not be your story . . . but maybe it is.

Or perhaps it's your scholastic journey. Maybe you've become addicted to earning degrees because you believe that more letters after your name provide the prestige necessary to matter.

Maybe it's your home. You don't much care about followers, but you do care that the home aesthetic you put out on your feed gets recognized. You want people who enter your home to see that Joanna Gaines has nothing on you. With each "ooh and ahh" that people offer on their trek through your castle, it gives you greater fuel to buy more and add more.

Or perhaps it's your job. You continue in this cycle of doing what-ever it takes, tiptoeing every ethical line you can, just to climb the next rung up the ladder. More promotion means a bigger platform, a bigger platform means that more people know you, and the more people that know you, the more sales you make. And of course, the more sales you make, the more money you bring in.

The common thread in all this?

Ambition.

While ambition isn't inherently evil, the motives driving our ambition can be.

We must grasp the truth about ambition as we wade through the life of our next Trailblazer. His words completely changed my life, moving my ambition from gaining fame to growing in faithfulness, from platform to purity, from charisma to character.

On that plane flying somewhere over the wide plains of Wyoming, I read these words from the apostle Paul: "Make it your ambition to lead a quiet life."[5]

The missing piece!

Could it be that to live a life like no one else means to ambitiously pursue a quiet life? In a world consumed by outrageous exploitation in a futile attempt to achieve fame, wealth, and status, could God really call us to quiet ambition, leading to a life of faithfulness, integrity, charity, and love?

Is such a life even possible? And if so, what does it look like in this day and age?

I now believe Paul's life provides a template for how to pursue a quiet, significant life. A life that, in retrospect, becomes a trailblazing story of consistency, curiosity, and character.

From Hypocrite to Hope Dealer

Paul, born Saul in the city of Tarsus, ended up apprenticing under one of Israel's most respected Rabbis, a scholar named Gamaliel. As a Pharisee, a religious expert in Jewish law, Saul saw it as his mandate to ensure the sanctity, purity, and preservation of Jewish religious customs.

Around the age of thirty, Saul witnessed the stoning of Stephen, a follower of Jesus. This tragic event sparked Saul's zeal to begin a campaign of persecution against Christians.

For some time, Saul went house to house, arresting Christians and transporting them back to Jerusalem for punishment. Soon, Saul's name became one of the most feared among early Christians.

During this season of life, Saul sought and gained permission to eradicate any evidence of the "Way [of Jesus]" from the synagogue at Damascus.[6] On his way to fulfill this mission—a mission that surely would have put his name even further on the map—he ran into Jesus himself.

> As he neared Damascus on his journey, suddenly a light from heaven flashed around him. He fell to the ground and heard a voice say to him, "Saul, Saul, why do you persecute me?"
> "Who are you, Lord?" Saul asked.
> "I am Jesus, whom you are persecuting," he replied.
> "Now get up and go into the city, and you will be told what you must do."[7]

At this point, Saul moved all his chips to the middle of the table. He was a highly esteemed Pharisee, persecuting and attempting to eradicate this wayward religious sect, and his fame, approval, and esteem had never risen higher.

When thinking about Saul the Pharisee, I recall the words of Jesus regarding prayer: "And when you pray, do not be like the hypocrites."[8] For a long time, Saul had flaunted his religious zeal like so many Pharisees—the way of the "hypocrite," as Jesus called it.

The other day, while scrolling on Twitter, I encountered one of the most uncomfortable videos I've ever seen. A group of young twenty-somethings aboard a full flight loudly sang, "How Great Is Our God" to a crowd of less-than-enthused people. At the time of this writing, that video had 32 million views and counting.

The more I watched it, the worse I felt.

While I'm all for evangelism, I have no interest in cornering people and shoving Jesus down their throats. Jesus issues invitations, he doesn't launch hostile takeovers. My friend Carlos offered his perspective, succinctly yet clearly: "This ain't it, Christian fam. This. Ain't. It."[9]

If we use the name of Jesus solely to create a viral video on TikTok, we are no better than the hypocrites who stood on Jerusalem's street corners praying only "to be seen by others."

Saul's encounter with Jesus changed everything. After three days of blindness, Saul repented and was reborn into a new life with Christ. Soon after, he began going by the name of Paul.[10]

Paul immediately went from hypocrite to hope dealer. His quiet, inner transformation speaks far louder than any of his zealous persecution campaigns ever did.

I find it fascinating *where* Paul went right after his conversion. This man with all the gifts, charisma, and resources to turn the ancient world toward Christ (as he soon does) doesn't go where we'd expect.

Someone with his résumé? After an encounter, conversion, and healing like that? That's a one-in-one-thousand sermon waiting to be preached. Surely, Paul would head straight for the temple in Jerusalem to begin preaching the gospel, right? Wouldn't that most honor God?

But Paul doesn't go there. Check this out:

> When God, who set me apart from my mother's womb and called me by his grace, was pleased to reveal his Son in me so that I might preach him among the Gentiles, *my immediate response was not to consult any human being. I did not go up to Jerusalem to see those who were apostles before I was, but I went into Arabia. Later I returned to Damascus.*
>
> *Then after three years, I went up to Jerusalem* to get acquainted with Cephas [Peter] and stayed with him fifteen days.[11]

Stun-ning.

Do you see it? The foundation on which Paul built his ministry?

Three years in the desert.

In obscurity. In the lonely place. In formation.

In *quiet*.

Paul commits the rest of his life to building the church of Jesus Christ. Through planting churches, training preachers and evangelists, taking three missionary journeys and writing fourteen (we think) New Testament epistles. Paul built his life around making the name of Jesus Christ famous. But he also built it on a foundation of quiet ambition. Rather than building his own status and fame, he surrendered to making the Lord's name great.

I probably should stop here to hammer out the rebuttal no doubt going through your mind: *But Micah, you just listed off a ton of things that Paul did that could have (and did) grow his fame in antiquity. Traveling, preaching, writing, planting churches—all of these things could have made Paul a big deal.*

And you know what? You're right.

But I hope you can see that a *quiet* life doesn't mean an *empty* life. To ambitiously pursue a quiet life doesn't mean to fail to make a difference or to have no influence in this world.

I think again of the words of John the Baptist about Jesus: "He must become greater; I must become less."[12]

To ambitiously pursue a quiet life means to, as clearly as possible, define what trail the Lord has called you to blaze, cheerfully traverse it, embrace your limits, and accept whatever comes with bringing all honor, glory, and praise to Jesus Christ alone. This doesn't mean the absence of accomplishing great things! Rather, it means accrediting any said accomplishments to Jesus Christ.

You faithfully blaze the trail, whether that's to impact ten people, ten thousand people, or ten million people, for as long as you possibly can, as well as you possibly can.

Paul modeled this for us when writing to the Corinthian church. Some of these people called themselves "super apostles" (think antiquity's version of "celebrity pastors").[13] Think people who use the name of Jesus to make a big deal of themselves.

Paul had credentials that matched or exceeded these individuals.

But what made Paul different is that in the end, the only thing he'd boast about is the Lord's grace, love, and mercy.

I know we're walking a fine line here. And I fully understand the potential for hypocrisy you may feel as you read a book that's been marketed to you for purchase. With whatever little relational equity I've built with you over the course of our time together, please know that I've labored over these words for hours upon hours, hoping and praying that I'd convey them in such a way that I communicate my true heart, and more importantly, that the Lord's truth would shine through.

I'm convinced of this: the difference between godly and worldly ambition comes down to *priority*. Does Jesus reign supreme? Or does your follower count, bank account, job position, reach, or platform reign supreme?

We can't know anyone else's heart, but we can take inventory of ourselves. We can take responsibility for ourselves.

I admit that a part of me wants my influence, popularity, and reach to reign supreme.

Acknowledging my sin and submitting to healthy accountability have helped to heal this hardened part of my heart.

So, with great fear and trembling, and with a humble limp acquired on my own trail, I seek to call *all* of us to a countercultural way of life. A life that ambitiously pursues quiet allegiance, a life in which Jesus reigns supreme. Let's receive our influence humbly as a gracious gift from the Lord, to be used to put the honor, glory, and recognition solely back onto him.

But . . . how do we do that?

Pursuing a Quiet Life

No bigger question has arisen for me in my apprenticeship to Jesus over the last three-plus years than this: "What does it look like to ambitiously pursue a quiet life?"

As a pastor and writer, aware of moving into the supposed "prime" years of youthful ambition, I've wrestled mightily with this question and others stemming from it.

"Does Paul call success bad?"

"Is it wrong for me to want great influence?"

"Should I delete social media forever?" (I wish, don't you?)

After studying and wrestling with the text, I've concluded that Paul's point doesn't focus on success, fame, or influence. In fact, you could be the CEO of a company of ten employees and live a "loud" life. You can also be a world-reaching writer and live a "quiet" life. The reach or influence you possess doesn't matter nearly so much as the heart posture with which you steward your influence.

I've gotten to know individuals who have hundreds of thousands of followers on social media. And yet, they're some of the healthiest, holiest, most humble people I know. On the other hand, I have many friends with hundreds or thousands of followers who act like they're above everyone in their path.

A quiet life stems from our integrity, not our level of impact.

Paul doesn't exhort us to non-activity but to live with character. Many men and women with unbelievable amounts of influence live "quiet" lives of integrity, faithfulness, and obedience to the trail God's called them to blaze. And many more scratch and claw for attention, fame, and acceptance, regardless of the compromises they make to attain such status.

So, what does it really mean to live a quiet life? I see three kinds of relationships we must have to blaze a trail with quiet ambition.

1. A core of fellow disciples

Every Trailblazer needs a core of individuals to help them remain rooted in their true identity. We need individuals who don't shrink from asking us the hard questions or from having difficult conversations. These people will travel with you to tough places, both literally and figuratively. Bluntly, we need people who will call us out when we start living sinfully, egotistically, or selfishly.

We see this kind of relationship core in the lives of both Paul and Jesus. Paul's core included Barnabas, Silas, Timothy, and Luke. These men journeyed, ministered, and lived with Paul for *years* at a time. Paul's relationship with each one is well-documented.[14] We also see Paul act as this type of friend for Peter.[15] Such a core beautifully expresses biblical accountability, without ever becoming Hollywood-esque. People in your core can be magnificently blunt and to the point while still expressing genuine love and respect.

Jesus' core included Peter, James, and John. Jesus handpicked these men to be present with him during many crucial moments of ministry.[16]

Do you have individuals willing to call you out of the dark and into the light? Do you have a core that helps you to live a quiet life?

2. Communities of support

Simply put, a community includes those people who do life alongside you. Who sits around the table with you?

Jesus modeled this practice throughout the Gospels. We see him gathering around the table with his twelve disciples as well as with the women who accompanied them. We also see Jesus gathering around the table with tax collectors, prostitutes, and other "sinners."[17] Perhaps surprisingly, we see the Pharisees—Jewish religious leaders, the best of the best in Jewish society—there too. His relational rhythm of gathering around the table lays out the blueprint for establishing authentic community.

Paul got extremely personal about those in his community. He names many of them: John Mark, Priscilla, Aquila, Onesimus and Tychicus, Aristarchus, Phoebe, and many more listed in the book of Romans alone.[18] Paul did life with these people, day in and day out. He shared stories with them, told them jokes, encouraged them, uplifted them, and prayed for them every day.

Can you see the commonality between Jesus and Paul? These communities featured men and women from different backgrounds, ethnicities, occupations, education levels, and socioeconomic statuses. They included powerful people and lowly people, people who supported them and others who dismissed them. They welcomed ancient-time conservatives and liberals, scoundrels and scholars, all gathered around the same table.

Despite the great impact that Paul and Jesus had on the world around them, their table reflected a community that made possible a quiet life.

They had no "green room" gatherings. They posted no VIP signs or guards at the door to determine which people seemed worthy to sit at the table. They intentionally issued an open invitation to reflect the nature of authentic community.

Diverse.

Nonstrategic.

Nonthreatening.

Simple.

Welcoming.

Warm.

Local.

May your table, your community—the people with whom you share meals in private—reflect this level of influence, care, tenderness, and compassion.

3. The local church

The church as Jesus meant it to be is a family. We belong to the local church as we belong to our families.

Paul's missionary journeys took him to the far corners of the ancient world and gave him the privilege of belonging to many church families. At every stop and each turn, he became rooted in that community, as his personal remarks to individuals in the book of Romans shows. We see this theme throughout all his letters to the churches (and families) to which he belonged. Whether at the church of Colossae, Rome, Ephesus, Corinth, or Philippi, he regularly worshiped with these people, prayed for them, ministered to them, and fasted and broke bread with them.

And for Jesus? Paul compared Jesus' relationship with the church to that of a husband and wife.[19]

The church offers each of us an opportunity to find community, love, and acceptance from and with one another and Christ himself. Within the church we learn to:

love one another;[20]

honor one another;[21]

build one another up;[22]

care for one another;[23]

serve one another;[24]

bear one another's burdens;[25]

forgive one another;[26]

and more.

For a long time, I interpreted Paul's exhortation to ambitiously pursue a quiet life as a command to do *nothing*. To have influence, to become broadly known, respected, or admired, and to live a public life, I thought, all opposed Paul's teaching.

But as I continued to study the lives of Paul and Jesus, I realized that any such interpretation had major problems. In fact, both had immense influence, both were (and are) broadly known, respected, and admired, and both lived incredibly public lives.

And yet, both lived *quiet* lives.

How can we reconcile public service with private obedience? Can the two coexist?

Yes, they can, through the common thread of doing life together.

With the critical relational layers in place—a core to be intimately known by, a community to do life with, and a church family to belong to—a very public life can draw from the deep well of a humble, rooted, private world.

Without humility comes humiliation. As the Scriptures clearly say, pride comes before the fall.[27]

But when we live life in authentic community, the people who love you can catch you before you hit the ground.

Character + Consistency = Clarity

What dream has God placed on your heart?

You may have ambitions to be the next president of the United States, to be first chair in the New York Philharmonic, to write a feature in the *New York Times*, or to have your own segment on ESPN or NBC *Nightly News*. The trail God calls you to blaze may thrust you into a spotlight of immense influence, fame, and popularity.

But with a core of people who know the real you, a community to do life with, and a church family to belong to, you can maintain a quiet life despite the vast amount of influence that God may bestow upon you. The seduction of fame has no power over anyone who has anchored their identity in Jesus Christ.

By contrast, your ambitions may lead you to far more local contexts. You may have in mind a life as a teacher, lawyer, pastor, business owner, cashier, stay-at-home parent, or accountant. You may never reach biography-status notoriety. And yet, the same lure of selfish ambition may entice you. The desire to make life about *us* exists no matter our occupation or social status.

Regardless of the position you find yourself in, ask yourself these questions:

Where do I want to go in life?

Why do I want to go there?

How is my core community shaping my character?

How curious do I get with those gathering around my table?

How consistently do I invest in my church family?

When you have clarity around these questions, you can begin to establish a firm foundation of integrity. The gap between your private world and public life begins to shrink, and who you are in every situation begins to look the same. *Exactly* the same.

Think of it like this:

$$Character + Consistency = Clarity$$

As the image gap shrinks, your life purpose expands. The very qualities of Jesus get infused, over time, into your heart and soul and lived out through your words and actions.

This kind of integration truly leads to a life like no other.

Displaying consistent character over time releases you to unapologetically blaze the trail God's entrusted you with, while remembering that the impact you make never has and never will be about you.

As Paul said in Romans 11:

To him be the glory forever! Amen.[28]

Amen.

13

LIVE LIKE JESUS

Holy

I LIKE ORDER.

By now, I hope we're on the same page about that. And if so, that makes the story of the *first* baptism of my brother Elijah and me that much better.

Yes, it was the first of many for Elijah and me. Now, before you theologically crucify me, know that these were not real baptisms.

One day, Mom was downstairs washing dishes after putting a bath on for my brother and me. Ten or so minutes later, she heard splashing, giggling, and the occasional "thump" coming from overhead. Curious, she slowly, quietly made her way up the stairs, rounded the corner, and peeked her head around the door.

"Elijah, do you confess with your mouth and believe within your heart that Jesus is Lord?"

Giggling "Yes."

"Well then, I now baptize you in the name of the Father, Son, and Holy Spirit."

Dunk.

Reversing roles now. Elijah—at three years old with a speech impediment—says it's my turn.

"Now, Micah."

"Yes?"

"Do you beweave that Jesus is Lord and that He died or your sins?"

"Yes."

"Well ven, I now baptize you in the name of the Ather, Son, and Holy Sthpearit."

Dunk.

This went on for another twenty minutes or so. Elijah and I experienced new life probably fifty or more times that day. Eventually, Mom couldn't contain herself and let out one of her signature cackles as she came to dry us off. She loves to tell that story of Elijah and me, five and three years old, in the tub in all our bare glory, baptizing each other over and over again.

We thought it was hilarious.

But deep down, I think another desire was at play.

Elijah and I desired *holiness*.

Because I like order, it's only fitting that we end our time together the way we should. Let's consider the overarching questions that ought to surround a work like this.

What's the point?

Why blaze a trail?

Why accept an invitation to a difficult, lonely, countercultural life?

Answer: to become *like Jesus*.

Is that not the goal of any person who wants to become a God-pleasing Christian? This trail we're blazing has an overarching destination: *holiness.*

Becoming *like* Jesus. Becoming whole, holy, and healthy people.[1] We become this type of person by looking back at the great saints of the Scriptures, echoing the character qualities they each modeled for us, and then looking to Jesus and witnessing how he embodied, perfected, and fulfilled these qualities during his life on earth. The apostle Paul put it this way: "Therefore be imitators of God, as beloved children. And walk in love, as Christ loved us and gave himself up for us, a fragrant offering and sacrifice to God."[2]

That is a life worth imitating.

So, let's take a closer look at the Savior of the world, Jesus Christ, the God-Man. He not only died, was buried, rose, and ascended into heaven, promising to return, but in his full humanity he showed us what the life of a Trailblazer truly looks like.

A Journey through Jesus' Life

Because I'm such a big fan of order, I want to journey through Jesus' life in the order of the individuals we've highlighted throughout this book. While we certainly want to emulate the good character traits these men and women possessed, we also recognize they share (along with us) a common thread of sin, mistakes, mishaps, and failure.

Not so with Jesus!

As the sinless Son of God, he perfectly embodied the good traits while never dabbling for a millisecond in the bad.

So, as we summarize the character attributes of these twelve Trailblazers, you'll quickly notice a pattern: Person A (Trailblazer) exhibited these traits in exemplary ways. Person B (Jesus) did so to perfection.

All right? Let's begin . . .

1. Joseph

A life of character forms in the wilderness. The wilderness took Joseph to the bottom of a pit, to Egypt as a slave, and to jail as a prisoner. There, God formed Joseph's godly character. There, God stripped away the teenaged Joseph's arrogance that had compelled the young man to joyously tell his older brothers of a dream in which they bowed down to him.

God formed Jesus' character in a wilderness too. Luke paints quite a picture:

> Jesus, full of the Holy Spirit, left the Jordan and was led by the Spirit into the wilderness, where for forty days he was tempted by the devil. He ate nothing during those days, and at the end of them he was hungry.[3]

After forty days of fasting in the wilderness, Jesus entered the crucible of character formation. Satan held nothing back, launching an all-out assault on Jesus' soul, using the three core motivators[4] of the human condition:

> to be useful;[5]

> to be important; and[6]

> to be powerful.[7]

Jesus overcame each of these assaults by reminding himself (and Satan) of the immutable truth of God's Word. And immediately after his battle in the wilderness, Jesus took initiative and stepped fully into the calling God had placed on his life.[8]

2. Abram

Full of faith, like Abram, Jesus began his own public ministry by visiting the synagogue in Capernaum on a Sabbath day. There he unrolled the scroll and preached from the book of Isaiah. "Today this scripture is fulfilled in your hearing," he told the astonished crowd.[9] No apprehension, no regret, and no apology.

God had called Jesus to blaze a unique trail. Jesus, in obedience and with full assurance, took initiative and proclaimed to the world that he, the Savior, had arrived. From "that very day,"[10] he was obedient to God's call, just like Abram was. Jesus began teaching the people about God's will and performing miracle after miracle. And yet unlike Abram, he did so without once stepping off the path God had laid out for him.

3. Moses

Whether Jesus drove out impure spirits, healed sickness and disease, provided food for large crowds in the wilderness, or raised people from the dead, his life overflowed with miraculous signs and wonders. Sound familiar?

Moses, too, performed many signs and wonders.

The difference?

Moses only reluctantly submitted to God's call as he battled insecurity, while Jesus confidently committed to blazing the trail God had called him to pioneer. No hint of insecurity. He knew he was God's beloved Son, in whom God was well pleased.[11] How beautiful that we now also possess that same secure identity as adopted sons and daughters of God!

4. Rahab

While Rahab bargained away her loyalty to secure safety for both her and her family, Jesus' loyalty came *at the expense of* his safety. Rahab's loyalty saved her life; Jesus' loyalty cost him his life (but through it gave us eternal life).

Jesus remained loyal to his disciples, even to Judas (whom he called "friend" even in the garden where Judas betrayed him)[12] and Peter (who denied him).[13] In the garden, "everyone deserted him and fled."[14] But despite their disloyalty to Jesus, he remained faithful and loyal to them.

And to *us*.

Looking past our betrayal, Jesus endured agonizing abuse from Roman soldiers and a shameful death on a cross . . . all out of loyalty, devotion, and an overarching commitment to lost men and women. That is, to us.

5. David

Where might Jesus' staggering strength come from? I see it born out of a threefold core of rhythms: solitude, slowness, and discipline. Much like David.

Jesus often retreated to a quiet place (*erémos* in Greek). The term can mean a lonely place, a desolate place, a deserted place, the wilderness, a secluded place, or the desert. In this desolate space, Jesus regularly went to commune in solitude with God the Father.

No Gospel writer captures this habit better than Mark.[15] Jesus repeatedly and intentionally got away from the noise, the distraction, and the busyness of life simply to *be* with God. Perhaps he experienced a unique level of clarity on the other side of his time in the *erémos*.

Clarity[16] in calling after spending time alone in the desert.[17]

Clarity in priority after withdrawing from large crowds.[18]

Clarity in perspective after mourning a loss.[19]

Clarity in decision-making in choosing his disciples.[20]

Clarity in resolve after wrestling with God's will.[21]

Jesus' life flowed out of a core foundation of solitude. He prioritized regular time with his Father. As solitude had formed and fashioned

David to serve as the king of Israel, so Jesus used solitude to form and fashion himself into the King of kings. But while David occasionally failed in his calling to shepherd the people he ruled, Jesus never once deviated from his calling as our Chief Shepherd.

6. Elijah

Jesus often moved slowly when others expected him to hurry. He was always intentional, present, attentive. He moved at an unbusy and unhurried pace.

Whether it be the woman caught in adultery, Jairus's daughter, or Zacchaeus the tax collector, time seemed to stand still in the way Jesus interacted with needy people. Jesus could do so by constantly giving a high level of attention to his inner spirit.

While it took an earthquake, a fire, and a great wind to get Elijah's attention and move him past the busyness, the noise, and the distractions of life,[22] Jesus consistently moved through throngs of people to attend to the needs of a single individual.

Where did that level of discernment come from? By listening for the still, small voice of God.

Jesus' life moved at the pace of the Father.

At the pace and rhythm of Love.

7. Esther

Speaking of rhythms, Jesus consistently engaged in the rhythm of fasting. Like Esther, Jesus used fasting as a vehicle for courage development. Esther held a three-day fast (nothing to sniff at) and on the other side of it found a vast amount of courage.

Jesus endured a forty-day fast. Think about that.

In the wilderness, subsequent to thirty years of obscurity and after fasting for forty days and forty nights—during which Satan tempted him to deviate from the path God had set out for him—Jesus finally stepped into public, full-time ministry.

For Esther, for Jesus, and for us, fasting functions like a strategic exercise of surrender. As we posture our whole selves—body, mind, heart, and spirit—before the Lord, he is faithful to fill us. As we let go of control, he imparts to us authentic, godly courage.

The courage cultivated in Esther through fasting allowed her to step before a ruthless tyrant and beg for the salvation of her people, even at the risk of her own life. The courage of Jesus allowed him to step faithfully toward Golgotha ("The Skull"), a trail that led to certain death on a cross. And yet, Jesus courageously stepped onto the path laid out for him and blazed the trail.

What drove him? His calling. *Nothing* could distract Jesus from what the Father had called him to do. And he chose that path freely, even though he knew it would cost him his life.

8. Daniel

The decisions we make have a direct impact on who we become. Like Daniel, Jesus had developed an inner strength to abide in God. But even Daniel didn't perfectly abide in the Lord, despite his great discipline. Like any mere human, he knew times of doubt, of selfishness, of sin. But until the terrible moment on the cross when he cried out, "My God, my God, why have you forsaken me?" he never experienced even a nanosecond of separation from the Father. As the Vine himself, Jesus knew what it meant to abide in his Father.

Daniel's discipline deeply embedded itself in him through his regular practice of the rhythms of a devout Jew: prayer three times a day, Sabbath, *kashrut* (food laws), memorizing the Torah, etc. This was Daniel's Rule of Life and although it did not give him continual communion with God, it did give him a deep spiritual life.

Similar practices such as solitude, silence, prayer, Scripture reading, Sabbath, community, eating and drinking, and more, comprised Jesus' Rule of Life. He always chose the *right* things, the *best* things, over and over again, which cultivated in him the discipline to live both intentionally and contemplatively. And through his Rule of Life, Jesus enjoyed *constant* communion with the Father.

9. John the Baptist

I've always admired Jesus' driven nature and singleness of focus. He had a masterful ability to remain committed to his calling while remaining totally present to people. I've often wondered how Jesus managed to balance these two tensions. I now believe he did so through his practice of simplicity.

To live simply is to live freely.

By disciplining himself to reject both worldly desires and materialism, Jesus could freely and intensely blaze the trail laid out for him.

Like his forerunner, John the Baptist, Jesus lived a simple life. Born into obscurity. Never had a family or owned a home. Never traveled more than 200 miles away from his birthplace. Yet out of that simplicity came an intensity of focus on the trail God had called him to blaze.

John, the one who prepared the way for Jesus, modeled this well. And yet, when John landed in prison for condemning King Herod's adultery, he wavered.[23] Things hadn't turned out as he'd expected. And so, he questioned whether Jesus really could be the prophesied Messiah.

Jesus *never* wavered.

Even in the garden, when he asked God for another way to save people other than through the cross, he remained committed to his Father's will. He would choose to blaze the trail all the way to Calvary.

10. The Apostle John

The disciple whom Jesus loved, the disciple so magnificently shaped and formed by the ethic of love, wrote his own account about what we call the Last Supper. The night before his death on the cross, Jesus stunningly took on the role of a lowly household servant and washed his disciples' feet. Despite having the most power, prestige, intellect, status, and authority in the room, Jesus humbled himself to teach his disciples yet another lesson in love.

John had a temper. Jesus had patience.

John displayed selfish ambition. Jesus embodied selfless submission.

John desired greatness. Jesus sought meekness.

John found his life when Jesus lost his.

The death, resurrection, and ascension of Jesus marked John so much that this "son of thunder" eventually became a savant on love. His three letters in the New Testament give us master classes on the subject.

Love one another. Outdo one another in service. Be humble. Be kind. Be gentle. Be present. John sometimes missed the mark on these things, but Jesus never did.

11. Peter

Peter's story provides us with a classic reminder of missing the mark. Repeatedly we see Peter fall short, and repeatedly we see Jesus invite him to try again.[24] Even when Peter loudly denied three times that he had any connection at all to Jesus, the Lord forgave him, accepted him, and commissioned him to blaze a trail that only Peter could.

Peter needed redemption. Jesus *is* redemption.

In the same way, Jesus' perfection overcomes our imperfections. His rightness outweighs our wrongness. His light outshines our dark.

12. Paul

The apostle Paul discovered the same grace and mercy that Peter did. Trying hard to build up his name, increase his approval ratings, and enlarge his profile, he violently persecuted the early church, trying to destroy it. Jesus interrupted his egocentric plans and transformed him into a man willing to endure incredible afflictions in his efforts to build up *Jesus'* name, esteem, and profile.[25]

In his apprenticeship to Jesus, Paul took to heart the charge of John the Baptist: "He must become greater; I must become less."[26]

In the quiet, backwards ambition of loving God and neighbor as himself, Paul changed the world for Christ (although he himself would write, "I will not venture to speak of anything except what Christ has accomplished through me in leading the Gentiles to obey God"[27]).

Paul understood that only Jesus *really* changes the world. And Jesus did change the world through his backwards ambition: even while "being in very nature God, [he] did not consider equality with God something to be used to his own advantage."[28]

Paul spent years building up his own platform, popularity, and power. Jesus spent years surrendering his own platform, popularity, and power. Our Lord "made himself nothing," "humbled himself," and "[became] obedient to death—even death on a cross."[29] In his quiet life, Jesus made the most noise of any individual in human history.

Consider Jesus

In character, courage, conviction, and commitment, Jesus perfectly fulfills the attributes of all the heroes of the faith that we admire.

Where they failed, he succeeded.

Where they fell short, he overcame.

Where they gave in, he endured.

Where they quit, he persevered.

Where they sinned, he obeyed.

All of this leads to a life of holiness. The all-encompassing, encapsulating life of Jesus embodies the very essence of holiness.

And his charge to us? "Go and do likewise."[30]

Resist the ungodly motivations of this world.

Obey the dream he's instilled inside your heart.

Blaze the trail.

Here's the Blueprint

What does it look like to live a holy, trailblazing life? The blueprint exists and is offered to us in, perhaps, an unlikely place.

You'll find it in Ephesians 5.

Ephesians 5?

Like the wedding passage (if you lean conservative)?

Or,

Like the oppressive call on women to submit (if you lean liberal)?

If you grew up in church and have an ounce of honesty in your bones, you can readily admit this passage carries some level of baggage for modern readers. But let's look beyond whatever angst this passage may bring.

Embedded in this passage, prior to the (what I've come to see as beautiful) instructions for marriage, lies a charge to a life of holiness for all of us.

Paul clearly lays out a template for a holy life beginning in verse 1: "Follow God's example, therefore, as dearly loved children."[31] Other translations say, "Be imitators of God," "Do as God would do," "Imitate God," and "Watch what God does, and then you do it."[32] And what does a life that imitates God, a life of holiness, consist of?

Here's our go-to passage:

> Among you there must not be even a hint of sexual immorality, or of any kind of impurity, or of greed, because these are improper for God's holy people. Nor should there be obscenity, foolish talk or coarse joking, which are out of

place, but rather thanksgiving. For of this you can be sure: No immoral, impure or greedy person—such a person is an idolater—has any inheritance in the kingdom of Christ and of God. Let no one deceive you with empty words, for because of such things God's wrath comes on those who are disobedient. Therefore do not be partners with them.[33]

Whoa. There's a lot here. Let's do our best to break it down succinctly.

"There must not be even a hint of sexual immorality."

Not even a hint?

Paul leaves zero room for misinterpretation. He charges "God's holy people" to lead the way in sexual integrity, to remain above reproach in every way.

How fitting is this word for our day? In a cultural moment where one study found that 91.5 percent of men and 60.2 percent of women have reported they've consumed pornography within the past calendar month,[34] how could we doubt that this passage applies to us?

In the digital age, where social media platform after social media platform comes saturated with sexual content, should we not do everything in our power and in our submission to Christ to live without "even a hint of sexual immorality"? How can we blaze a holy trail if we fail here?

This is not easy. And it will not happen if we just "try."

But it is possible.

My own journey with sexual immorality led me to understand that through the power of the Holy Spirit—and with accountability, guardrails, wisdom, and discernment—the fight to root out sexual immorality (*porneia* in Greek) can be won, every day.[35] But it all comes back to the gift that God gave us in the garden at the beginning of time.

Free will. A choice.

We must choose.

Will we choose sexual immorality or sexual holiness?

We cannot faithfully and fully blaze the trail God has asked us to blaze if we continually compromise ourselves sexually. The life of a Trailblazer is a life set apart, a life that chooses the way of Jesus over the ways of the world—*especially* (and in this culture, primarily) in the area of sexuality.

> *"Nor should there be obscenity, foolish talk or coarse joking, which are out of place, but rather thanksgiving."*

I find it interesting that Paul doesn't counter obscene, foolish talk with wise or uplifting talk but rather with thanksgiving.

We love to grumble. If we're not careful, we can always find something to complain about. We live in a time when things like cancel culture, road rage, and obscene language have become the norm. Putting others down and silencing them has become a part-time job for many of us, and the use of degrading, hurtful, vile language has become our primary weapon.

Thanksgiving is different.

Thanksgiving is the front door to right speech. All we must do is put it into practice.

Wanna try?

Right now, think of five things for which you're grateful. As you reflect, your body will begin to relax, your mind will slow down, and joy will fill your heart.

Thanksgiving language is centering language. It reorients our perspective. As our minds fix on the things, people, or places that God has graciously given to us, the exercise transforms our heart posture.

And the result? *Holy language.*

One best-selling author said it best: "I never met a bitter person who was thankful. Or a thankful person who was bitter."[36]

As we grow in thanksgiving, we increase space for humility, peace, hope, and love to permeate our spirit and root out bitterness, jealousy, obscenity, and vileness. Grateful language is holy language.

As we pursue a life of holiness, let's make gratitude ever-present on our lips.

> "For of this you can be sure: No immoral, impure or greedy person—such a person is an idolater—has any inheritance in the kingdom of Christ and of God."

Idolatry is a painful substitute for God.

The tragic story of the Israelites wandering in the desert warns us about people who bow to idols rather than to God. Thousands of years later, things haven't changed.

Many of us are wandering, struggling, feeling hopeless about the direction of our lives.

A *New York Times* article recently used a single word to describe the American people in a post-COVID-19 pandemic world: "Languishing."[37]

Yikes.

Adam Grant, the article's author, defines languishing as "a sense of stagnation and emptiness. It feels as if you're muddling through your days, looking at your life through a foggy windshield."

So, what do we do?

Many of us have turned to our vice of choice—drugs, alcohol, pornography, Netflix, TikTok, whatever our idol may be—to fill the empty, languishing void in our hearts.

Paul's invitation to a life of holiness comes down to a simple binary: Will I place my hope and trust in (fill in the blank) or will I find my hope and trust exclusively in Jesus Christ, the Son of God?

Paul says that a life of immorality, impurity, greed—of living a life in submission to idols—rips away the eternal inheritance of the Kingdom of God. What do we do with that?

We *choose.*

Day after day, week after week, we choose to submit to God the world's empty promises, pleasures, and profits. We surrender our desire to escape and instead run into the arms of our loving Father. We give up our desire for lustful pleasure and instead fill ourselves with the life-giving joy of Jesus.

We choose to declare, "No more idols!"[38] We drop them at the foot of the cross and live in submission and obedience to Christ alone. As we root out the idols in our lives and pattern our ways after Jesus, we develop a healthy life.

A holy life.

> *"Let no one deceive you with empty words, for because of such things God's wrath comes on those who are disobedient. Therefore do not be partners with them."*

We can view much of this from a negative standpoint.

"There must not be."

"Let no one."

"Do not."

Strong language, to be sure. But it's also straightforward. Paul wants to be clear: to live a life of holiness, we must reject unholiness. We must not allow "empty words" to deceive us. And the false promises of our world pop up everywhere.

We live in a culture and age where to be flashy is to flourish.

To be successful is sexy.

To be wealthy is winning.

To be an influencer is inspiring.

To be famous is fruitful.

And to be notable is noble.

Do you see all the unhealthy motivators at play here?

This, we're told constantly, is the *good* life. A life of worth. Of value. Of prestige. Of significance.

But we serve a God who exhorts us to make it our ambition to lead a quiet life. To refuse to center our lives around ourselves but to center them around loving God and our neighbor as ourselves.[39]

Such a life requires a departure, a de-partnering if you will, from individuals who subscribe to the ways of the world.

Does this mean we stop loving others? No, of course not.

But we do draw a line in the sand. We understand that to live a life like no one else, we must . . . well . . . *live a life like no one else's.*

It may seem trivial, but it's imperative to understand this. We cannot passively consecrate ourselves or be set apart. Say it with me: *we must choose.*

Will we indulge in the ways of the world or will we steadfastly pursue a life of "follow[ing] God's example," of being "imitators of God"? Of living a *holy* life?

You must make your choice.

Hear this, please, as a gentle invitation: Are you tired? Weary? Burdened? Jesus says, "Come to me. I'll give you a real rest."[40]

Do you want that? I know I do.

By the blood of Jesus and through his sacrifice on the cross, victory over death, and ascension into heaven, we have been invited to participate in the redemptive pursuit of humanity.

Not as perfect vessels, but as purchased sons and daughters.

You Matter to God

Your life matters. No matter the cards you've been dealt or the circumstances you find yourself in, you matter to God. All of us need the call he's placed on our lives and the trail he's called us to blaze.

In a world obsessed with careerism, we need people devoted to character first.

In a world of passivity, we need people who take initiative.

In a world of fear, we need people who trustingly submit.

We need individuals willing to fight against the diseased motivators of shame, noise, hurry, hatred, and selfish ambition.

We need people willing and ready to be set apart in the pursuit of holiness.

As you move, God will assure. He hasn't called you to blaze this trail by accident.

Don't run from it, embrace it.

Don't apologize for it, accept it.

Don't discredit it, acknowledge it.

Step onto the trail, full of faith, believing that who God has called you to be is exactly who you are.

What's your dream? As we close our time together, allow it to sit at the top of your mind.

MY DREAM:

_____

_____

_____

_____

_____

_____

_____

_____

_____

Now, step into it. Full of faith, hope, and love.

Look to the figures of the past and embrace the best of what they had to offer. Notice how God used them in mighty ways, despite their many flaws.

God wants to use you, *all* of you—your flaws, your failures, your fears, your doubts, your strengths, your gifts, your talents, and your abilities—to change this world. To help bring heaven on earth.

You have what it takes. Now, it's time.

Are you ready?

Go, and be the Trailblazer God has called you to be.

I'll see you at the finish line.

WALK THE WALK

"SO, LIKE, THEORETICALLY, if we were to plant a church . . . um, would you be up for us using your building?"

For weeks, I felt tormented by this nagging sense that God was leading Rylei and me to plant a church.

Surely not, I thought. *Me? There's no way, God.*

After a few weeks of going back and forth, I finally caved. I texted my friend, Oscar, to see if he'd be up for grabbing lunch. We met at Super Tacos on a Tuesday afternoon. We sat down and I started stirring my straw *slowly*.

Oscar pastors a Methodist church on our street corner. His Hispanic congregation lies well outside the scope and stream of the kind of Christianity I knew growing up. But still . . . I couldn't shake this feeling that I needed to ask him.

So, I asked him.

"Sure," he replied, "I don't see why not."

Strike one.

I went home and asked Rylei if she wanted to go for a walk. She did.

"So, like, theoretically, if we were to plant a church . . . would you, um, be up for that?"

"Sure, I don't see why not."

Strike two.

Over the course of the next month, the urge only grew stronger. In May of 2022, Rylei and I both, separately, felt as if we'd received a specific invitation from the Lord:

"Pastor your neighborhood."

We had no idea what that meant, but we decided to press in.

That summer, we spent an exorbitant amount of time retreating from the normal rhythms of our day-to-day life in search of God's voice. Remember, it's often in the quiet spaces—not the earth-quakes, winds, or fires of life—that God speaks.

We decided to create space.

"Speak, for your servant is listening."[1]

On June 23, 2022, one day before Rylei and my fourth wedding anniversary, two different pastors approached me about possibly planting a church—one in Indianapolis, the other in Grand Rapids, Michigan.

Perhaps I should mention that Rylei's parents live in Grand Rapids. Oh, and the location where we'd plant? Knapp Street, the very same street where my in-laws have lived for the last twenty-five-plus years. "Our" neighborhood.

We decided to pray about it.

The following month, we spent a weekend celebrating our birth-days and anniversary at a cabin in the woods, the perfect place to unhurriedly meet with God.

"Speak, for your servant is listening."[2]

Two days in, Rylei came downstairs after her morning quiet time. "I think we're supposed to stay in Indy," she said.

"I think so too," I replied.

When we returned home, I made the call. We'd officially decided to plant a church in our neighborhood, in Indianapolis. We felt thrilled! God had set a trail for us to blaze. We readied ourselves to step in.

But then, a haunting question hit me: *Now what? I don't know what I'm doing.*

That thought struck me two months ago. And you know what? I *still* don't know what I'm doing.

But God often works like that, doesn't he? He invites us to live out whatever he's forming in us. In other words, he calls us to practice what we preach. He wants us to exercise faith, give generously, praise frequently, pray continually, and surrender repeatedly.

He asks us to walk the walk.

How Did We Get Here?

How did Rylei and I get here? Our lived experience brought us to this precipice, to this fork in the road moment—a "forever afterwards" mile-marker as we continue to move forward.

Frankly, I have no idea if we'll succeed. I have no idea if this church plant will grow or die, thrive or merely survive, make an impact or just scrape by.

But I do know that the Lord has extended an invitation to us: "Pastor your neighborhood."

We've had to make the choice to obey that call. Would we give up all the comfort and ease of our familiar life and radically trust in the character of Jesus Christ?

We said, "Yes."

Rylei has quit her job as a teacher and has taken on a new assign-ment that gives her more flexibility and freedom to do ministry. I've quit my job as a high school pastor and have stepped into the role of pastor of teaching and vision for The Sanctuary: A Neighborhood Church. We're made up of a local group of radical ordinaries seek-ing to restore Indianapolis as it is in heaven.

Sound a little pompous? Perhaps. But the size of the dream doesn't even come *close* to the size of our God. His ways, his provision, and his character *massively* surpass anything we could ever dream.

So, in humble obedience, we've said, "Yes." Even if we can't see where the trail ultimately leads.

What About You?

This, I hope, is the best part of what you've read in this book. I hope you haven't walked through these pages thinking I'm some sort of "expert" on Trailblazing. Nothing could be further from the truth!

Frankly, I've written this book, not *to you* but *for us*. Jesus himself extends to us all an invitation to step into life, life to the full. What will we do with that invitation? And where do we go from here?

What does it mean for you to be an authentic follower of Jesus in your city, in your context, in this cultural moment?

That question has kept me up at night for *years*.

And as I've labored to find the answer, it's brought me here, to the precipice of blazing an exciting new trail. We're striving together to partner with God to form and fashion a brand-new community of believers. We long to reach a previously unreached people group for Jesus. And God is using us to form a catalytic community of people of all shapes, sizes, races, and ages. Men and women, boys and girls, from various backgrounds, socioeconomic statuses, and family structures. A community of like-minded individuals who have committed themselves to practice the Way, participate in missional community, and permeate the world.

What about you?

My friend, it's time to take the dream out of the secret place and into the public square. The time has come for you to take a risk, to make a move, to accept the invitation.

Most of us, of course, rarely make progress without some healthy accountability keeping us on track. Who's ever lost an exorbitant amount of weight, paid off a hefty amount of debt, or achieved a difficult accomplishment, without a coach, trainer, or advisor in their ear along the way?

Sheer willpower won't blaze the trail for you. Moses had Aaron; Esther had Mordecai; and even Jesus had James, John, and Peter.

Who will it be for you? Who's going to join you on this journey of trailblazing?

Life to the full waits for you. But will you choose to accept it?

A Way-Too-Big Dream

I hope you've conjured up a dream that scares you to death. Why? Because Satan so often uses fear to enslave us and drive us to safe, ordinary, mundane lives.

Now, please don't mishear me. There's beauty in the ordinary. In fact, much of the Christian life is normal, mundane, even boring. The normalcy of life presents us with a great gift. And if you find yourself in that space right now, rejoice!

But my experience tells me that even in the Ordinary Time, *something* is always coming. We see this every year in the cycle of the church calendar. Pentecost precedes Ordinary Time while Advent follows it. The coming of the Holy Spirit and the arrival of Jesus Christ sandwich Ordinary Time, year in and year out.

Yes, something is *always* coming.

Every now and then, an invitation arrives, an opportunity to step off the ledge of the safe, secure life you've built and to step into a previously unexplored, new depth of faith. This is the way of the Trailblazer.

And Jesus routinely and gently extends to us an avenue of release from our overreliant selves, along with a radical reignition of our longing for God. In these fork-in-the-road moments, Jesus intimately fashions Trailblazers.

Over the course of a lifetime, such catalytic incidents become altars of remembrance. Perhaps the trail ahead calls you to . . .

- apply to that law school
- move to that country
- propose to that woman
- start the business
- call and ask for forgiveness from that child

Whatever the "it" is for you, the time has come. Don't wait! Apply, move, propose, start, call. What's holding you back?

When I achieve this GPA . . .

When I secure this job . . .

When I have more in the bank . . .

When I make it through Thanksgiving . . .

Recognize each of these as excuses. They come disguised as distractions, designed to keep you from stepping into your true purpose. Too often, we allow the weight of distraction to keep us from the trail that God has called us to blaze.

Our digital age itself tends to distract us out of our purpose. Tech company *TeamStage* did an intense study on distraction in the workplace. It found that:

> Fifty percent of employees say that they feel distracted by their phones at work.
>
> Ninety-eight percent of the workforce say they get interrupted at least three or four times a day.
>
> Distractions can lead to committing twice as many errors as usual.
>
> It takes twenty-three minutes and fifteen seconds to fully recover focus after a distraction.[3]

Distraction has infiltrated our day-to-day lives so deeply that we now accept it as normal. And yet, because of it we make costly mistakes, dig ourselves into ruts, and miss out on maximizing our potential—all in the name of "not missing out."[4]

Surrounding circumstances also keep our dreams at bay. Now, I know that some have been systemically or unfairly dealt a bad hand. That is wrong and I'm sorry if the game of life has disadvantaged you. As a middle-class white man, I recognize how easily so many opportunities have come my way. I've also persevered through and overcome a great amount of adversity throughout my life.

No matter where you've started, you have a big part in determining where you finish. To each of us, Jesus extends an opportunity to grow past our circumstances, whether financial, spiritual, emotional, physical, or whatever.

C. S. Lewis brilliantly put it this way:

> If we let ourselves, we shall always be waiting for some distraction or other to end before we can really get down to our work. The only people who achieve much are those

who want knowledge so badly that they seek it while the conditions are still unfavourable. Favourable conditions never come."[5]

Are you waiting for the "perfect" moment to step into your calling? If so, prepare yourself to wait a lifetime.

You must decide whether or not you'll go after whatever God has imprinted on your heart. And once you decide to step out and blaze the trail, know that distraction will not disappear. Its tempting presence, in fact, will only increase. I say this not to discourage you but simply to name reality and to challenge you to know that the true character of a Trailblazer gets tested in this very arena.

Consider each day an opportunity to partner with Jesus to bring heaven on earth.

But you must choose.

What Will You Choose?

Will you cave in to the way of the world? Or will you follow the Way that is Jesus?

Trailblazers practice unrelenting commitment in a world of abrupt abandonment.

Trailblazers exercise communal interdependence in a world of ravenous individualism.

Trailblazers practice unrivaled allegiance in a world of transient loyalty.

Trailblazers say "Yes" to the difficult Way of Jesus in a world eagerly seeking the easy way out.

At every turn, at every fork, you will have to make a choice. Will you become a countercultural Trailblazer? Or end up a casualty of distraction?

Jesus, through the power of the Holy Spirit, offers you and me the chance to overcome. To conquer. To persevere, so that his name may be exalted above every other name.

Can't you see it? At the name of Jesus, *every* knee will bow and *every* tongue confess that Jesus is Lord, to the glory of God the Father.

To all of us he says "Come and follow me." Follow Jesus into the life you've always wanted to live!

You ready? We have trails to blaze.

Acknowledgments

This book is the sum total of various kind, intelligent individuals who believed that the way of the Trailblazer was a message worth hearing. Writing a book is a laborious, time-consuming, pedantic process. It goes in starts and stops, over months (in this case, *years*), distilling ideas into actual words on pages. The book you've just read has come a long way from its initial genesis in my head. To those who were part of that process, I am forever grateful.

To Thomas Sisson: You were the first person to believe in me. The first to tell me that I could do this. That I could be a Trailblazer like the people I felt compelled to write about. I am forever grateful for your belief in and support of me. Love you so much.

To the high school students of Northview Church, who lived out this vision for the very first time in 2020—the year we all took up the mantle of blazing new trails: What a joy and privilege it was to be your pastor during that time.

To Andy and Candace Stephenson: Thanks for teaching me what a true vision day is supposed to be—unhurried time with the Father, Son, and Spirit. Those days have become my most protected over the years.

To David Henderson, for mulling over these ideas at length via Zoom: I'm grateful for your decades of faithfulness to the pastorate.

To Dick and Sibyl Towner and the Springs staff: Sitting under your spiritual direction in the "quiet place" has been transformative from the inside out.

To Dan Balow, for taking a chance on me: Thank you for being patient, kind, and supportive. Here's to the next one.

To the Tyndale Team, for also taking a chance on me: Sarah Atkinson, Alyssa Clements, Stephanie Rische, and countless others who made this book come to life. What a joy it was to labor alongside each of you. To Kara Leonino: Thank you for making the process fun and exciting. In you, I felt I had my biggest fan. Special thanks to Steve Halliday for helping my writing to reach its ceiling. You are a gift, my friend.

To Eric Simpson, for teaching me about liminal space: I cherish our times in your office among the great fathers and mothers of faith.

To the many mentors and voices of truth in my life who have modeled this for me: Steve Carter, Dr. Derwin Gray, Annie Downs, Daniel Grothe, Scott Sauls, Jenni Wong Clayville, Mark Malin, and Kent Bjurstrom. I'm so grateful for each of your voices in my life. Thanks for going first.

To the Northview Students Team: You all lived this out alongside me years ago. Special thanks to Zach, Jenn, Caleb, Kylee, and Devyn—each of you were in my ear constantly with encouragement, support, and challenge when needed. I cherish our time serving alongside one another.

To the Brotherhood: Somehow God brought us together from all over the world to cheer, support, and spur one another on through this incredibly beautiful, difficult call of pastoring. I'm thankful for the faithfulness, grace, and drive you each model. You've made me a better pastor. Our safe place has become sacred space in my life.

To The Sanctuary: We're blazing trails in real time. I'm not even sure where we'll end up, but I know that with God ahead, behind, above, below, to the right, and to the left, it's going to be beautiful.

May we be a people who continually push to live by the values of heaven, for the sake of the world.

To our covenant community: Hirsches and Siewerts, we've been through it all together. You have taught me about the incredible reward that's received when the fight to be fully known and fully loved is won. I love doing life with you guys.

To my family: Walsh fam, thank you for opening up your home for many early-morning writing sessions, for being a safe place to be myself, and for allowing me to marry your daughter/sister. Elijah, Isaiah, Jailyn, and Janiyah: There are few titles I wear more proudly than "big brother." I'm so proud of each of you and who you're becoming.

To Mom: For inspiring me to write beautiful words. To Dad: For inspiring me to preach them. You guys have been my model for basically everything. Thanks for doing the hard work of unwinding so much generational sin so that we could live a better way.

Last, to Rylei: How do I encapsulate the love I have for you? I'm unable. So I'll simply tell you that I love you, till death do us part. You are my rock, my best friend, and my muse. Life as I knew it radically changed when you came into the picture. I wouldn't have it any other way. Here's to the future—blazing trails side by side for decades to come. You forever have my heart.

Discussion Guide

1. Years ago, Micah's pastor challenged him to set aside time to have a "vision day." How could you apply this challenge to your life and what might a "vision day" look like for you?

2. Micah says there are two types of motivators that people face in life—heavenly ones and worldly ones. How can heavenly motivators impact or change your life?

3. The life of a Trailblazer consists of opportunities to say yes to the future God has in store for you. Can you think of a time in your life when you felt God wanted you to do something that would help you move closer to a goal or dream? If so, how did you respond in that situation?

4. What can a person do if they experience insecurity and doubt while attempting to try something new?

5. In chapter 4, Micah says that when people pledge loyalty to Jesus, they end up surrendering things the world deems valuable. What worldly things might you be called to surrender to show your loyalty to Jesus?

6. What are some benefits of having times of solitude?

7. In chapter 6, Micah mentions learning about the idea of hurry from Pastor John Mark Comer and says his challenge to overcome hurry is to "embrace our limits and then lean into . . .

a 'slow-down spirituality'." What could this challenge look like in your life?

8. Is there anything in your life that you could put on pause for the moment so that you don't get burned out?

9. Esther is seen by many as a biblical role model for how to live courageously. What lessons can you take from Esther's story that can be applied to your circumstances?

10. Think for a moment about a dream or goal that you have. What could you do today to courageously move one step closer to realizing it?

11. In chapter 8, Micah provides a list of spiritual disciplines or "rhythms" that individuals can practice to help them become the person they are meant to be. Which one or more could you start practicing in your life today?

12. What are some things you could do to live a simpler life moving forward?

13. Showing love to others may require us to push aside feelings of embarrassment or doubt. Describe a time when someone risked being embarrassed to help you or a loved one.

14. In chapter 11, Micah encourages us that we can still blaze a trail even if we have failed. Of the four actions Micah describes needing to take place for us to keep moving forward (repentance, commitment, acceptance, and forgiveness), which feels the most daunting for you and why?

15. Micah says that the difference between godly and worldly ambition comes down to one word: *priority*. What things are taking priority in your life, and would you categorize them as godly or worldly ambitions?

16. In what ways are you and your local church practicing authentic community based on the list Micah provides in chapter 12? What do you think you are doing well and what do you still need to work on?

17. The character of different biblical Trailblazers was put on display in this book. Which Trailblazer's story resonated with you the most? Is there anything from their story that you believe will help you blaze your own trails?

Notes

PROLOGUE: WHAT IS A TRAILBLAZER?

1. A mentor of mine, Eric Simpson, first introduced me to the concept of liminal space.

2. Theodora Blanchfield, "What is Liminal Space? A Transitional Place or Time that Can Feel Unsettling," Verywell Mind, September 19, 2022, https://www.verywellmind.com/the-impact-of-liminal-space-on-your-mental-health-5204371.

3. Adam Grant, "There's a Name for the Blah You're Feeling: It's Called Languishing," New York Times, April 19, 2021, https://www.nytimes.com/2021/04/19/well/mind/covid-mental-health-languishing.html.

4. A phrase from my hero, Eugene Peterson. I'll quote this again later.

5. Here's just one example: Guardian of Valor Stolen Valor, "Fake Marine Called Out by Army Officer in Kansas Airport Stolen Valor," video, 2:25, https://www.youtube.com/watch?v=rbkB8Rf6b2U.

6. See Jesus' teaching in Matthew 7 for more on this.

CHAPTER 1: BUILD A FOUNDATION OF INTEGRITY

1. Genesis 45:5.

2. Genesis 37:3.

3. Pretty sure this word was first used in Justin Bieber's heartthrob single, "Boyfriend." I'm proud to admit this is no longer in the normal stream of my vocabulary.

4. Merriam-Webster, s.v. "ornate (adj.)," accessed November 10, 2022, https://www.merriam-webster.com/dictionary/ornate.

5. Genesis 37:5-11.

6. Genesis 37:12-24.

7. Genesis 37:26-27.

8. The full account of Joseph and Potiphar's wife can be found in Genesis 39.

9. For the full story, see Genesis 40.

10. This transformative exchange in Joseph's life is recounted in detail in Genesis 41.

11. The exchange between Joseph and his brothers can be found in Genesis 42–45.

12. Genesis 45:5.

13. Genesis 50:20.

14. *Merriam-Webster*, s.v. "character (*n.*)," accessed November 10, 2022, https://www.merriam-webster.com/dictionary/character.

15. James Merritt, *Character Still Counts: It Is Time to Restore Our Lasting Values* (Eugene, OR: Harvest House, 2019), 15.

16. Merritt, *Character Still Counts*, 21.

17. One of the few Christian clichés I cling to. I'll try to keep them to a minimum, I promise!

CHAPTER 2: TAKE THE FIRST STEP

1. We're camping out for now in Genesis 12:1-4.

2. Genesis 12:1.

3. Genesis 12:2-3, my paraphrase.

4. Genesis 12:4.

5. See Genesis 12:4 for the specific reference.

6. I don't drink, but as I write this, it's thirty-four degrees and snowing here in Indianapolis. What I'd give to be anywhere south!

7. This happens during Abram's name-changing in Genesis 17.

8. I say "traditional" because Abram by this point had a son, Ishmael, out of wedlock with a female slave named Hagar.

9. Genesis 17:17.

10. Genesis 21:6.

11. Most scholars believe Jesus fulfilled at least 300 prophecies during his time on earth. Alfred Edersheim, in *The Life and Times of Jesus*

the Messiah (1890), found 456 Old Testament verses referencing the coming of Jesus.

12. Joshua 24:2, ESV.

13. Walter A. Elwell, *Evangelical Dictionary of Theology* (Grand Rapids, MI: Baker Academic, 2003).

14. Genesis 12:1-3.

15. Genesis 15:18-21.

16. Genesis 17:2-9.

17. Many of these promises aren't fulfilled until the life and times of Joshua, almost 450 years later.

18. The two stories appear in Genesis 12:10-20 and Genesis 20.

19. Genesis 12:4.

20. Genesis 13.

21. Genesis 14.

22. Genesis 19:1-29.

23. Genesis 19:30-38.

24. Full story in Genesis 16.

25. Love you so much, Steve Carter.

26. See God to David in 2 Samuel 12:7-8 for yet another example of this.

27. Genesis 17:1-6.

28. See Romans 4:19; Hebrews 11:11.

29. Genesis 17:5-6.

30. Genesis 17:10-11.

31. Genesis 17:15-16.

32. Genesis 17:17-18.

33. Genesis 17:19-27.

34. Most historians agree that Ishmael was the patriarch of Qedar, an ancient Arab tribe. Some have gone as far as to say that Ishmael was the father of Islam and an ancestor of the prophet, Muhammad, though that hasn't been proven to be true.

35. This refers to the promise God makes to Abraham's son, Isaac, in Genesis 26:4.

CHAPTER 3: FAITHFULLY FIGHT INSECURITY

1. My parents expound more on this in their own book, *Beyond Ordinary*. Justin Davis and Trisha Davis, *Beyond Ordinary: When A Good Marriage Isn't Good Enough* (Carol Stream, IL: Tyndale, 2012).

2. Exodus 2:1-10 shares in detail Moses' fortune.

3. Exodus 2:11-21.

4. Exodus 3:4-7.

5. Exodus 3:11.

6. Exodus 3:13.

7. Exodus 3:14.

8. Exodus 4:2-9.

9. Exodus 4:13.

10. Matthew 26:37.

11. Matthew 26:39.

12. Benjamin William Hastings, vocalist, "Homeward," by Bryan Fowler, Benjamin William Hastings, and Ben Fielding, release date October 14, 2021, track 9 on *Benjamin William Hastings*.

13. You can find the real Prodigal Son story in Luke 15.

14. Numbers 6.

15. Matthew 6:10.

CHAPTER 4: DEVOTED AT THE RIGHT COST

1. Statista, "Number of Civilian Casualties in Ukraine during Russia's Invasion Verified by OHCHR as of November 27, 2022," accessed December 1, 2022, https://www.statista.com /statistics/1293492/ukraine-war-casualties/.

2. Valerie Hopkins, "In Video, a Defiant Zelensky Says, 'We Are Here,'" *New York Times*, February 25, 2022, https://www.nytimes.com /2022/02/25/world/europe/zelensky-speech-video.html.

3. A strong group culture is anchored by habits, norms, traditions, or values, which in turn shape the individuals who make up the broader group. A great read on this is Joseph Hellerman, *When the Church Was a Family: Recapturing Jesus' Vision for Authentic Christian Community* (Nashville, TN: B&H Academic, 2009).

4. "Mahatma Gandhi," History.com, June 6, 2019, https://www.history .com/topics/india/mahatma-gandhi.

5. "Michael Jordan on Being Cut from High School Varsity: 'I Just Wasn't Good Enough.'" Oldskoolbball.com, April 7, 2020, https://oldskoolbball.com/michael-jordan-high-school-varsity/.

6. Bill Zehme, "Tom Hanks Is Mr. Big" *Rolling Stone*, June 30, 1988, https://www.rollingstone.com/tv-movies/tv-movie-news/tom-hanks -is-mr-big-73890/.

7. Michael Ray, "Volodymyr Zelensky: President of Ukraine," *Britannica*, September 30, 2022, https://www.britannica.com/biography /Volodymyr-Zelensky.

8. Joshua 2:1.

9. Joshua 2:2.

10. Joshua 2:4-7.

11. Joshua 2:8-12.

12. Rahab makes a deal with the spies in Joshua 2:12-16.

13. Luke 14:33.

14. Galatians 5:22.

15. 2 Corinthians 12:10.

16. I heard this in a message from Pete Greig at New Life Church. New Life Downtown, Pete Greig, "How to Hear God," June 19, 2022, video, 1:35:42, https://www.youtube.com/watch?v=LjHBlcgGboE.

17. Eugene Peterson, *A Long Obedience in the Same Direction: Discipleship in an Instant Society* (Downers Grove, IL: InterVarsity, 2000).

18. Matthew 1:5-6.

19. I first discovered this tool in Peter Scazzero, *Emotionally Healthy Discipleship: Moving from Shallow Christianity to Deep Transformation* (Grand Rapids, MI: Zondervan, 2021).

CHAPTER 5: LEARN TO BE ALONE

1. The Springs in Oldenburg, Indiana, has become a second home to me. Dick and Sibyl Towner and David Henderson have become spiritual fathers and a spiritual mother in my life.

2. This was pre-streaming services; Redbox was still a thing.

3. For purposes of length, I'm not including the part of that conversation where I was told to be home right after and that I was grounded.

4. I believe in and have experienced communal conversations with the Spirit and don't want to negate that aspect of the faith.

5. Psalm 1:1-3.

6. Psalm 8:1.

7. Psalm 9:1-2.

8. Psalm 10:1.

9. Psalm 15:1.

10. Psalm 15:2-5.

11. Psalm 23:1-6, emphasis added.

12. This being Eugene Peterson.

13. Psalm 23:2, MSG.

14. Matthew 11:28-30, MSG, emphasis added.

15. Scripture refers to God's voice as a still, small voice in an interaction the prophet Elijah had with God, described in 1 Kings 19:11-12, NKJV.

16. 1 Samuel 3:10.

CHAPTER 6: DECELERATE AND LISTEN

1. This quote can be found in John Ortberg, *Soul Keeping: Caring for the Most Important Part of You* (Grand Rapids, MI: Zondervan, 2014), 20. I read it for the first time, however, in John Mark Comer, *The Ruthless Elimination of Hurry: How to Stay Emotionally Healthy and Spiritually Alive in the Chaos of the Modern World* (Colorado Springs, CO: Waterbrook, 2019), 19. Both are must-reads. Both have been so formational for me personally.

2. You can find the meat of it in 1 Kings 17–19.

3. 1 Kings 17:1.

4. 1 Kings 17:2-6.

5. 1 Kings 17:7-16.

6. 1 Kings 17:17-24.

7. 1 Kings 18:16-24.

8. 1 Kings 18:30-38.

9. 1 Kings 18:40.

10. 1 Kings 19:1-2.

11. 1 Kings 19:3-5.

12. If you need reading recommendations, I recommend anything this man writes.

13. Matthew Lapine, "Forget Charisma. Look for the Weak and the Slow," *Christianity Today*, Fall 2022, https://christianitytoday.com/pastors/2022/fall/forget-charisma-look-for-weak-and-slow.html.

14. Kosuke Koyama, *Three Mile an Hour God* (London: SCM Press, 2015), 7.

15. Matthew 16:26.

16. Comer, *Ruthless Elimination of Hurry*, 23.

17. 1 Kings 19:5-9.

18. 1 Kings 19:9.

19. 1 Kings 19:10.

20. 1 Kings 19:11-13.

21. 1 Kings 19:13-14.

22. 1 Kings 19:15-21.

23. G. E. Miller, "The U. S. Is the Most Overworked Developed Nation in the World," 20 Something Finance blog, January 30, 2022, https://20somethingfinance.com/american-hours-worked-productivity-vacation/.

24. Cal Newport, *Digital Minimalism: Choosing a Focused Life in a Noisy World* (New York: Portfolio/Penguin, 2019), 109.

25. Here's the original article: Melissa Kirsch, "Change Your Screen to Grayscale to Combat Phone Addiction," Lifehacker, February 18, 2020, http://lifehacker.com/change-your-screen-to-grayscale-to-combat-phone-addicti-1795821843.

26. Maria Clarke, "19 Negative Effects of Technology on Mental Health," Etactics, June 3, 2021, https://etactics.com/blog/negative-effects-of-technology-on-mental-health; "Screen Dependency Disorder: The Effects of 'Screen Time' Addiction," Neurohealth, February 11, 2020, https://nhahealth.com/screen-dependency-disorder-the-effects-of-screen-time-addiction/.

27. Genesis 2:1-3.

28. Mark 2:27.

CHAPTER 7: ALWAYS CHOOSE TO BE BRAVE

1. Clayborne Carson, ed., *The Autobiography of Martin Luther King, Jr.* (New York: Warner Books, 2001), 88.

2. Carson, 79.

3. Carson, 80.

4. Esther 2:1-18.

5. Esther 1:10-22.

6. Esther 2:10.

7. Esther 3:1-15.

8. Esther 4:13-15, emphasis added.

9. Indiana Wesleyan University in Marion, Indiana. You'll always have a place in my heart.

10. That would be Lincoln, Illinois. You too, have a place in my heart, dear Lincoln Christian University.

11. Esther 4:13-15, emphasis added.

12. Esther 4:14.

13. Esther 4:16.

14. Genesis 16:13.

15. Esther 7:1-4.

16. Esther 7:5–8:4.

17. Esther 8:7-14.

18. Esther 8:15-17.

19. Scot McKnight, "Fasting: A Technique?" Patheos, March 22, 2007, https://www.patheos.com/blogs/jesuscreed/2007/03/22/fasting-a-technique/.

20. Matthew 4:2.

21. Jesus, on the eve of his crucifixion, prays, "Father, if you are willing, take this cup from me; yet not my will, but yours be done" (Luke 22:42).

22. John 16:33.

23. I know, another cliché. I'm sorry!

CHAPTER 8: TAKE CHARGE OF YOUR DAY

1. That's "T" as in Tonagel—Greg Tonagel, one of the greatest small college basketball coaches of all time and a man who has had a profound spiritual influence in my own life.

2. A hilarious article in *USA Today* is worth the read: Charles Curtis, "Kawhi Leonard Explains His Weird 'Board Man Gets Paid' Trash Talk," For the Win, *USA Today Sports*, June 6, 2019, https://ftw.usatoday.com/2019/06/nba-finals-kawhi-leonard-board-man.

3. Francesca Donovan, "This Is How Much of Your Life You've Spent on the Toilet," Unilad, last updated April 9, 2021, https://www.unilad.co .uk/featured/this-is-how-much-of-your-life-youve-spent-on-the-toilet.

4. Another phrase I love from my mentor, Steve C! Love you, Carter!

5. Romans 12:2, ESV.

6. This is an ode to my Art of Teaching crew. ☺ Grateful for you, Tyson!

7. Daniel 1:3-4.

8. Daniel 1:8.

9. Daniel 1:13.

10. Daniel 1:15.

11. Daniel 6:3.

12. Daniel 6:7.

13. Daniel 6:10.

14. Daniel 6:19-23.

15. Gerald L. Sittser, *Water from a Deep Well: Christian Spirituality from Early Martyrs to Modern Missionaries* (Downers Grove, IL: InterVarsity, 2010), 37.

16. *The Acts of the Christian Martyrs,* quoted in Sittser, *Water from a Deep Well*, 38.

17. Sittser, 39.

18. Sittser writes much about Perpetua's commitment to prayer, singing the Psalms, showing mercy to guards, and living kindly in her last days in prison. Perpetua's devotion to Jesus stemmed from a deep-rooted commitment of faith.

19. To all of the mega-reformers: I'm not suggesting the Desert Fathers and Mothers were perfect. I know they got a lot wrong. I'm simply saying that the church at large needs to recapture something like practicing a Rule of Life.

20. Esther de Waal, *A Life-Giving Way: A Commentary on the Rule of St. Benedict* (Collegeville, MN: Liturgical Press, 2014), ix.

21. John 15:5.

22. By experts, I mean pastors, monks, and mystics—people who are far smarter, wiser, older, and have much more experience than I have.

23. Micah E. Davis, "A Guide to Crafting a Rule of Life" e-book, www.micahedavis.com/ruleoflife.

CHAPTER 9: UNCOMPLICATE LIFE, GAIN SUBSTANCE

1. Esther de Waal, *The Way of Simplicity: The Cistercian Tradition* (New York: Liturgical Press, 2010).

2. Charles Dumont, "Contemplative Action: Time in Eternity according to St. Bernard," *CSQ* 28 (1993.2), 156.

3. De Waal, *Way of Simplicity*, 21.

4. Luke 3:1-2.

5. Luke 3:3; Matthew 3:1-2; Mark 1:4.

6. Luke 3:21; Matthew 3:16; Mark 1:9.

7. Mark 1:6.

8. Elizabeth Fletcher, "Clothes for Rich and Poor," Women in the Bible, http://womeninthebible.net/bible-archeology/clothes_rich_poor/.

9. Mark 1:6.

10. Luke 1:11-15, emphasis added.

11. Luke 1:80.

12. Matthew 3:3, citing Isaiah 40:3.

13. Luke 1:13-17.

14. Luke 1:76-77.

15. John 3:28-30.

16. John 3:30.

17. Richard Foster, *Freedom of Simplicity: Finding Harmony in a Complex World* (San Francisco: Harper, 2005), 9.

18. Mary MacVean, "For Many People, Gathering Possessions Is Just the Stuff of Life," *Los Angeles Times*, March 21, 2014, http://articles.latimes.com/2014/mar/21/health/la-he-keeping-stuff-20140322.

19. Jon Mooallem, "The Self-Storage Self," *New York Times*, September 2, 2009, www.nytimes.com/2009/09/06/magazine/06self-storage-t.html?_r=0.

20. Matthew 6:21.

21. Joshua Becker, *The More of Less: Finding the Life You Want Under Everything You Own* (Colorado Springs, CO: Waterbrook, 2016), 18.

22. 1 Timothy 6:6-7.

23. Sarah Butler, "H&M Factories in Myanmar Employed 14-Year-Old Workers," *Guardian*, August 21, 2016, https://www.theguardian.com

/business/2016/aug/21/hm-factories-myanmar-employed-14-year
-old-workers.

24. https://goodonyou.eco/.

25. 1 Timothy 6:6.

26. Galatians 5:22-23.

27. Thomas R. Kelly, *A Testament of Devotion* (San Francisco: HarperCollins, 1996), 124.

28. John 3:30.

CHAPTER 10: LOVE (PERIOD)

1. Genesis 1.

2. If you're looking for a resource on the Sabbath, I'd highly recommend Wayne Mueller's book by the same title. It has been extremely formative in my own view of Sabbath. Wayne Mueller, *Sabbath: Finding Rest, Renewal, and Delight in Our Busy Lives* (New York: Bantam, 2000).

3. This was ingrained into me through John Mark Comer's chapter on "slowing" in his book, *The Ruthless Elimination of Hurry: How to Stay Emotionally Healthy and Spiritually Alive in the Chaos of the Modern World* (Colorado Springs, CO: Waterbrook, 2019).

4. Luke 4:12.

5. As Paul notes in 1 Corinthians 13:2.

6. Mark 3:17.

7. Mark 5:37; Matthew 17:1-13; Matthew 26:37.

8. John 19:26.

9. Most sources I drew from stated that the book of 1 John was written sometime between AD 85 and 95. Here's one such source: "Intro to 1 John," Biblica, https://www.biblica.com/resources/scholar-notes/niv-study-bible/intro-to-1-john/.

10. 1 John 2:1.

11. 1 John 1:7.

12. 1 John 2:3-6, emphasis added.

13. John 15:1-4.

14. I pulled these cross references from a document I found by Mark Allan Powell. Insights are my own. Here's the link: Mark Allan Powell, "Similarities between the Johannine Letters and the Gospel of John"

(Baker Academic, 2009), http://assets.bakerpublishinggroup.com/processed/esource-assets/files/657/original/27-02.pdf?1417315445.

15. 1 John 2:9-11.

16. John 8:12.

17. 1 John 3:11.

18. John 15:1-17.

19. 1 John 3:13.

20. John 15:18-19.

21. 1 John 3:16-18.

22. John 10:11, 15, 17-18.

23. John 15:12-13.

24. John 13:23 for just one reference.

25. Mark 10:35-45.

26. Matthew 20:20-28; some scholars believe this is the same one recounted in Mark 10:35-45, just through a different lens.

27. John 20:8.

28. As quoted by John Mark Comer in "Interview with John Mark Comer," The Carey Nieuwhof Leadership podcast, transcript accessed December 1, 2022, https://careynieuwhof.com/wp-content/uploads/2020/01/CNLP_316-%E2%80%93With_John-Mark-Comer.pdf.

29. The full exchange can be found in Matthew 22:36-40.

30. Matthew 22:37-39.

31. 1 John 4:8.

32. 1 Corinthians 13:4-7, NLT.

33. 1 John 3:17.

34. Matthew 16:24.

35. John 3:16.

36. 1 John 4:13-21.

37. 1 John 4:13-21.

38. Matthew 22:36-40.

CHAPTER 11: NEVER GIVE UP

1. *Merriam-Webster*, s.v. "failure (*n.*)," accessed November 10, 2022, https://www.merriam-webster.com/dictionary/failure.

2. Lestraundra Alfred, "55 Inspirational Quotes about Learning from Failure," HubSpot, March 11, 2022, https://blog.hubspot.com/sales/learning-from-failure-quotes.

3. Luke 5:8.

4. Luke 5:10.

5. Matthew 16:13.

6. Matthew 16:14.

7. Matthew 16:15, emphasis added.

8. Matthew 16:16.

9. Matthew 16:17-18.

10. Luke 22:54-62.

11. Luke 22:62.

12. This is an excerpt from my parents' beautiful book: Justin Davis and Trisha Davis, *Beyond Ordinary: When a Good Marriage Isn't Good Enough* (Carol Stream, IL: Tyndale, 2012). It's worth reading in its entirety, but this passage comes from page 152 (emphasis added).

13. Matthew 7:13.

14. Luke 24:12.

15. Luke 24:12.

16. See John 21.

17. He said it in his 2022 Easter sermon; at lunch that day I told him I'd steal it. Thanks, Dad!

18. John 20:19-20.

19. John 20:26-27.

20. 2 Corinthians 5:17.

21. Davis, *Beyond Ordinary*, 160, emphasis added.

22. Davis, *Beyond Ordinary*, 180–181.

23. John 21:15-17.

CHAPTER 12: LEAN INTO BACKWARDS AMBITION

1. Aishwarya Dharni, "Social Media Fame: Absolutely Crazy Things People Did to Get Famous on the Internet," India Times, February 13, 2021, https://www.indiatimes.com/trending/wtf/crazy-things-people-did-for-social-media-fame-534216.html.

2. See Andy Crouch, *The Tech-Wise Family* (Grand Rapids, MI: Baker Books, 2017) and Cal Newport, *Digital Minimalism* (New York: Penguin, 2019).

3. Gen Z lingo for "a fake person" or computer.

4. David D. Luxton, Jennifer D. June, and Jonathan M. Fairall, "Social Media and Suicide: A Public Health Perspective," *American Journal of Public Health*, April 12, 2012, https://ajph.aphapublications.org/doi /full/10.2105/AJPH.2011.300608.

5. 1 Thessalonians 4:11.

6. Acts 22:3-5.

7. Acts 9:3-6.

8. Matthew 6:5.

9. Carlos Whittaker (@loswhit), "This. Is. Embarrassing. Had these been Muslims praying loudly I GUARANTEE there would have been handcuffs and swearing. This ain't it Christian fam. This. Ain't. It." Twitter, April 16, 2022, 4:07 p.m., https://twitter.com/loswhit/status /1515436692290912262?s=20&t=ZDNsnvx9OCSSWUxhZOnhhQ.

10. Acts 13:9.

11. Galatians 1:15-18, NIV, emphasis added.

12. John 3:30.

13. I think we should parse out what kind of "celebrity pastor" we have in view here. Many pastors become public figures based on influence, not by choice. This is not wrong nor should it be held against these individuals. Others, however, get so ingrained in the fame game that their congregation becomes a means to an end of personal gain. I'm sure we all know the difference.

14. Acts 13; Acts 16; 1 and 2 Timothy.

15. Galatians 2:11-13.

16. Mark 9:2-3; Luke 8:49-56; Matthew 26:36-38.

17. Luke 5:29; Luke 7:37-39.

18. Marg Mowczko, "A List of the 29 People in Romans 16:1-16," Marg Mowczko blog, May 18, 2019, https://margmowczko.com/list-of -people-in-romans-16_1-16/.

19. Ephesians 5:22-30.

20. John 13:34.

21. Romans 12:10.

22. Romans 14:19; 1 Thessalonians 5:11.

23. 1 Corinthians 12:25.

24. Galatians 5:13.

25. Galatians 6:2.

26. Ephesians 4:2, 32; Colossians 3:13.

27. Proverbs 16:18.

28. Romans 11:36.

CHAPTER 13: LIVE LIKE JESUS

1. A line from my guy Steve Carter.

2. Ephesians 5:1-2, ESV.

3. Luke 4:1-2.

4. These are adapted from Henri J. M. Nouwen, *In the Name of Jesus: Reflections on Christian Leadership* (New York: Crossroad, 2015).

5. Luke 4:3-4.

6. Luke 4:5-8.

7. Luke 4:10-12.

8. See Luke 4:14-15.

9. Luke 4:16-21.

10. See Genesis 17:23 and Abram's response to God's call.

11. Luke 3:22.

12. Luke 22:3-6; Matthew 26:49-50.

13. Luke 22:54-66.

14. Mark 14:50.

15. Mark 1:35, 45; 3:7; 6:31; 6:46.

16. Adapted from Ward Cushman, "There's a Place for Solitude in All Our Lives," To Every Nation, https://toeverynation.com/6-times-when-jesus-chose-solitude-over-people/.

17. Luke 4:1-2, 14-15.

18. Mark 6:30-32.

19. Mark 14:1-13.

20. Luke 6:12-13.

21. Luke 22:39-44.

22. See 1 Kings 19:11-13.

23. Matthew 11:2-15.

24. I know the theology of all of this can get wonky quickly. Please, don't see this as a pass to pursue some antinomianism. I hope by this point we're on the same page: living in obedience to the way of Jesus. But I'm not God and neither are you. Time after time (Acts 15:11; Romans 3:24; Titus 2:11; Ephesians 2:8-9, etc.), we are told that if we put our faith and hope in Jesus, his grace wins out in the end. That's why I believe Jesus offers *all* of us second, third, and fiftieth chances. I stand by that.

25. See 2 Corinthians 11 for his résumé.

26. John 3:30.

27. Romans 15:18.

28. Philippians 2:6.

29. Philippians 2:5-8.

30. Luke 10:37.

31. Ephesians 5:1.

32. Ephesians 5:1, ESV, NLV, NLT, MSG.

33. Ephesians 5:3-7.

34. "How Many People Are on Porn Sites Right Now? (Hint: It's a Lot.)," Fight the New Drug, April 5, 2022, https://fightthenewdrug.org /by-the-numbers-see-how-many-people-are-watching-porn-today/.

35. I've made so many mistakes in this area throughout my life. I was a virgin at my wedding altar by the skin of my teeth. My twisted, I-kissed-dating-goodbye ideal instilled in me as a child kept me from going "all the way" in bed with another woman prior to marriage, but it didn't keep me from giving myself fully to pornography, manipulating multitudes of women, and for years engaging in a plethora of disturbing acts and decisions. I share all of this to simply say, if you have been or are currently engaged in sexual sin—no shame from me. I've needed a lot of healing in this area of my life. But now, after years of freedom, fidelity, and faithfulness to one woman, I've just begun to scratch the surface of what a life of genuine sexual integrity holds. And it is glorious. It is freeing. It is everything that Jesus promised it'd be. It's worth the effort. Get help. Reach out. I'm with you!

36. Attributed to Nick Vujicic, QuoteFancy.com, https://quotefancy.com /quote/876124/Nick-Vujicic-I-never-met-a-bitter-person-who-was -thankful-Or-a-thankful-person-who-was.

37. Adam Grant, "There's a Name for the Blah You're Feeling: It's Called Languishing," *New York Times*, April 19, 2021, www.nytimes.com /2021/04/19/well/mind/covid-mental-health-languishing.html.

38. An incredible song by Impact Music if you're looking for a great worship song to add to your worship playlist. https://www.multitracks .com/songs/Impact-Music/No-More-Idols/.

39. Matthew 22:37-40.

40. Paraphrase of Matthew 11:28-30, MSG.

EPILOGUE: WALK THE WALK

1. 1 Samuel 3:10.

2. 1 Samuel 3:10.

3. "Workplace Distractions Statistics: Problems and Solutions in 2022," TeamStage blog, https://teamstage.io/workplace-distractions -statistics/.

4. I once had a conversation with a high school junior who averaged ten hours of screen time per day on her device. "I can't miss out," she told me. "If I'm sent a text, DM, or Snap, I have to know immediately what's said."

5. C. S. Lewis, *The Weight of Glory* (New York: HarperCollins, 2001), 61.

About the Author

MICAH E. DAVIS lives and writes inside "the loop" of Indianapolis, Indiana, with his wife, Rylei, and their Australian Kelpie, Leo.

He is the pastor of teaching and vision at The Sanctuary: A Neighborhood Church. Micah believes the written and spoken word are mediums to elicit heart change and life transformation. He has committed his life to using words for good.

For more of Micah's teachings on faith, formation, and the life of Jesus, go to sanctuaryindy.com and sign up for the podcast, or visit micahedavis.com.

Facebook, Instagram, and Twitter: @micahedavis